Sex in Islam and other worldviews

Sex in Islam and other worldviews

Towards a Global Sexual Ethos

Derek Kelly, Ph.D.

Writers Club Press
San Jose   New York   Lincoln   Shanghai

Sex in Islam and other worldviews
Towards a Global Sexual Ethos

Writers Club Press
an imprint of iUniverse, Inc.

For information address:
iUniverse, Inc.
5220 S. 16th St., Suite 200
Lincoln, NE 68512
www.iuniverse.com

Anyone interested in how human sexual expression
is viewed in various religions

ISBN: 0-595-21178-X

Printed in the United States of America

For Robin, Earth Mother

Contents

Preface

Whatever the topic, whether it is attraction, procreation, same-gender sexuality, monogamy, or whatever, people around the world rarely discuss sex in an open manner. We humans spend a good amount of time dealing with and pondering topics about sex and sexuality, yet frank and honest talk about sexual matters is hard to find anywhere. And if sexual activity is a controversial issue for discussion in society and our daily lives, it is no less so as a topic in political and legal communities.

The Sexual Taboo

Some years ago during the Clinton Administration, then Surgeon General Jocelyn Elders suggested that one way of reducing the increase in out-of-wedlock births among minority, mainly black, women was to teach them how to masturbate. This would help prevent them from ending up pregnant, poor or diseased. Clinton, no doubt in part because he was already up to his ears in sexual problems, fired her.[1] End of subject. End of discussion.

A few years later, David Satcher, Surgeon General, issued a report on human sexuality and the Bush administration was very distressed with him. Why? Among other reasons, because he had opened the possibility that homosexuality was an ingrained, genetic condition and this went against the grain of the ayatollahs in the congress, who champion the idea

---

[1] See http://www.equityfeminism.com/75—.

of getting homosexuals to change their ways. He also advocated certain new ideas for combating AIDS.[2]

Human sexual expression in general is something few people in this society, in fact few people in the world, wants to talk about. Just about everyone on the face of this planet finds some way of shying away from the subject, or some way of shunting the subject off to something peripheral. Though there are numerous social problems with a basis in sex practices—AIDS, overpopulation, environmental degradation—very few people around the world ever raise the issues to a level of discussion; and if they do, they are soon blotted out by enormous silence or ostracism.

For example, Daniel Arap Moi, President of Kenya, suggested in July 2001, that Kenyans should avoid having sex for two years (what he meant was sex involving intercourse) so as to stem the tide of AIDS. One of his countrymen was reported to have said: "You have to have sex, those who will die will die, and whoever does not get AIDS, then good for him."[3]

Advancing celibacy as a solution to AIDS is in itself laughable, but at least Moi was making an effort to address a problem. Had he, instead, suggested that Kenyans engage in as much sex as they wanted, only that they limit it to themselves (auto-amore), not only would he have had a realistic solution to the AIDS problem, but he would also have been roundly condemned by the powerful Catholic church in Kenya, and ridiculed by his fellow citizens. Why is this the case?

Aims of the Book

I have several aims in writing this book. As I noted above, talking about the forms of human sexual expression is taboo among the world's cultures

---

[2] See http://www.cnsnews.com/indepth/archive/199807/IND19980-701g.html.

[3] See http://www.guardian.co.uk/aids/story/0,7369,521239,00.html.

and civilizations. Oh, for sure, we talk about sex; men are notorious for talking about their real or imagined sexual conquests and about the sexual preferences of those who are thought of as queer in some way. Many of our advertisements are blatantly sexual in nature as are our TV shows and movies. But talking dispassionately or objectively about sexual forms is not something that people seem willing to do. One aim of the book is to open the matter to discussion.

Another aim is to contribute to the social, political, cultural, religious, and philosophical debates that divide and alienate us from each other. On a symbolic level, it appears that many of the divisions among human beings are caused by cultural, ethnic, and ideological differences. One of my convictions is that underlying all social arrangements are sexual passions and attitudes, and that just about every problem can be reduced to its sexual components. I am equally convinced that we can resolve many of our differences by a dispassionate discussion about sex.[4]

Underlying all forms of sexual expression are worldviews (also known as belief systems, ideologies, or religions). I have selected six worldviews—Buddhism, Christianity, Hinduism, Islam, Paganism and Taoism—as the prisms through which to look at the modes of sexual expression. Once having delineated the characteristics of "acceptable" sexual expression within each of these worldviews, I then attempt to develop a common sexual ethos for humanity. So, a final aim of the book is to provide an avenue for reconciling the diverse views of sexual expression and of the cultures into one, expansive and embracing concept.

Who this Book is for

This book is for every human being on the planet, now and in the future. It is for religious leaders; a goodly portion of the book is devoted to

---

[4.] See Antony Grey, *Speaking of Sex*, London: Cassell, 1993. Grey, an avowed homosexual, describes attitudes toward sex in Great Britain, but he could just as easily have been talking about the USA.

a consideration of sexual expression in six of the world's major worldviews[5]. It is for philosophical leaders; again for the same reason. It is for politicians and legislators who propose laws governing forms of sexual expression. It is for social workers. It is for ordinary men and women worldwide who seek some way of ameliorating the human condition.

Organization

I begin the discussion by talking about the sexual "itch." We need to acknowledge that this itch is one of the strongest and most basic needs in the human makeup. Our social and political arrangements are governed by how we understand and deal with that itch.

I next move to a consideration of the forms (and within the forms, the modes) of sexual expression. My intent here is to develop a set of what Max Weber called ideal types, fundamental forms, of sexual expression. These forms are cast as independent of the sexes, that is are independent of whether or not males or females are involved, and are also cast as independent of the value-laden terms we use to talk about sexual expression.

Following that, I take a look at the views of sexuality advanced by six of the world's culturally extensive worldviews—Buddhism, Christianity, Hinduism, Islam, Paganism and Taoism. These worldviews were selected because each one forms the basis of life or is followed by at least one billion people, making them the worldviews of well over 90 percent of the world's people. Some people would argue that underlying all religions or worldviews is Paganism—and that we are all Pagans. This would, in effect, mean that I have considered the worldviews of all of the world's people.

Only after we understand the metaphysical foundations of the social systems favored by the greater majority of the world's people will we be in

---

5. I am using the word worldview instead of religion or belief system since a religion usually has a theology of sorts and rituals of worship of some divine being, yet Buddhism, for example, certainly does not.

a position to understand the acceptable and unacceptable forms of human sexual expression—and be in a better position to understand the opposition to various logically legitimate forms of human sexual expression.

It is at this point that I will turn to a consideration of the social, political, and medical problems whose solution can be found in various forms of human sexual expression. In the course of the argument, I will suggest that if we are to have a genuine associative or confederated global society, we must move beyond and away from the traditional religions, and toward a new sexual ethos based on a more realistic view of sexuality.

Sources and Conventions

Several coined terms are used throughout the text. Instead of "monogamy," I use the term "mono-amore" to indicate one-to-one loving, which may or may not have legal sanction. Instead of polygamy, I use the term poly-amore for the same reason. Also, I use the term auto-amore for sexual activity that involves only one person.

In the West, we refer to the holy scriptures of the Islamic religion as the Koran. However, Muslims refer to the book as the Qur'an. Here I refer to it as the Quran.

Up until the last year or so, it was common to talk about sexually transmitted diseases (STDs). I have adopted the more recent reference as sexually transmitted infections (STIs).

Since so many of us are "on" the Internet these days, I include both books and URLs among my sources.

Introduction

This book is about what has been called the primal urge and a small set of logically distinct ways in which the primal urge may be satisfied. To avoid getting us off the track, this introduction will define the sexual urge and the context within which it will be considered in the book.

The Sexual Instinct

Instincts and appetites are ingredients of all life on earth. Common to both animals and humans alike are sense impulses and biological urges. All animals, it appears, and certainly humans, have been endowed by the creator or by evolution, take your pick, by an urge that is governed in both men and women by the hormone testosterone. Those people who have lost their desire for sexual release can find it again with a dose of testosterone.

The sexual appetite, whatever its biological or metaphysical basis, is one of the most prominent, important and essential aspects of human, animal and plant life. The sex instinct is certainly one of the greatest urges in human life. Sex energy or lust is a deeply rooted instinct in humans. Sex energy is constantly on the mind, and affects the senses of the entire body. The sex impulse is a most demanding craving among humans.

The views and interpretations of the sex instinct are quite varied. The views range all over the map and include everything from simple physiological urges to the grandest of metaphysical schemes where the sex drive and the will to live, even the world will, are identified. In this section, I wish to describe three of the most basic views about the sex instinct so as to demarcate the view I have adapted for the purposes of this book from these other views.

Schopenhauer and the Copulation Principle

Arthur Schopenhauer was a philosopher who ruminated about sex and sexuality in a book describing the nature of the world, which he described as being will and idea. Schopenhauer regarded sex as the "lord of the world."[6] While we may think that sexuality is simply the product of the instincts and drives of life, Schopenhauer saw it as an embodiment of the "will" of the world, a sort of blind drive inherent to the universe as a whole.

Schopenhauer sees procreation as the aim of sex. Individuals may think they are happy because they have sex, but in fact sex is the way the world's will assures that reproduction will take place. People begin in an act of copulation and spend their lives desiring copulation.[7]

Like Freud after him, Schopenhauer sees sexuality as pervasive in all human motivation. The sex drive springs from the depths of our nature. For most humans (man in the natural state) sex is life's final end and highest goal—it is in fact the most demanding of all cravings. Schopenhauer finds sex at the basis of most human activities—jokes, allusions, war, peace, creation, and general existence. Sex is in fact the ultimate goal of all human effort.[8]

Frankly, Schopenhauer is not as radical as he may appear—and in some cases, he's definitely wrong. That the sole purpose of sex is procreation is not at all obvious. The sole purpose of the itch is satisfaction, release. If it happens that the release takes place in a suitable vessel (a female), procreation may result, but more often than not, it does not result in procreation. Similarly, while we may be products of copulation, and may desire release from the itch, copulation is by no means the sole way in which this

---

[6] See Arthur Schopenhauer, *The World as Will and Representation*, Volume 2, Translated by E.F.J. Payne, New York: Dover, 1966, p 513.

[7] Ibid, p 514.

[8] Ibid, pp 513-514.

may be accomplished. Women having sex with other women do not necessarily copulate, certainly not in the sense meant here. And men having sex with men do not procreate.

Freud and the Erotic Principle

Though there is ample evidence that Freud was heavily influenced by Schopenhauer in his views of sex, I think that Freud did not go as far as Schopenhauer in extending sexuality as a manifestation of the will of the universe, but was satisfied to limit it to pleasure-seeking in general and then further reduced pleasure-seeking to a universally pervasive erotic principle governing all life.

Freud claimed that the principal motives of all mental and cultural (including economic) work are the instincts. We humans are driven by an infinitely large number of instincts[9] all of which can be reduced to two principal ones. One is Eros, the life instinct, and the other is Thanatos, the death instinct.[10]

Eros, the life instinct, is the principle that governs all the forces that seek life, build structures and synthesize the varied features of our psychic lives. Eros, exemplified most clearly in the sexual drive, is universal. The sexual drive is not only or even primarily genital pleasure, but is the basis of all pleasure seeking whatsoever. Hence, he even identified what he called infantile or pre-genital sexuality, which is a drive conditioned by Eros even

---

[9] We know that each gene in the human genome is a little actor that performs a single function. I suppose Freud's view of the infinity of instincts could be reduced to the finite number of genes in the genome, substituting the word instinct for gene.

[10] See Freud's 1905 book, *Three Essays on the Theory of Sexuality*. In light of the discoveries concerning the pain and pleasure centers in the brain, as described by Arthur Janov in *The Biology of Love*, New York: Prometheus, 2000, perhaps Freud might have been on the right track for it seems that the pain centers are of two types, morbid and life-denying.

if it is not genital in nature. Similarly, he claims that sexual energy (libido) is the single most important motivating force in adult human life.

Sex as Genital Pleasure

Whether or not sexuality is one of two fundamental principles of life (Freud) or is the will of the world seeking copulation (and procreation) as its fundamental purpose are views that are far too metaphysical and abstract for my purposes. I will grant that sex is a systemic—that is, pervasive—phenomenon, but it would serve no purpose of get embroiled in controversies that are far beyond the scope of this book.

That is why I wish to define the sexual urge simply as an urge that normal humans (and other animals may) have on a regular (often daily) basis for some release from the build up of the sexual fluids. Put another way, I wish to define the sex instinct simply as a physiological demand for genital release and (maybe) pleasure. When there are itches on the body, mere scratching of them is a pleasure. The sex impulse is like a nervous itching. The satisfaction of this impulse begets pleasure, or at least release from the itch. Whether or not this urge is an urge of the universe or based on some pleasure-seeking principle is not my concern here.

The release of sexual fluids and the possibly accompanying pleasure[11] have a certain pattern in normal humans, which are in men arousal, erection, ejaculation, and orgasm. Women follow a similar pattern, though erection for them may be in the clitoris and nipples rather than in the penis. So, what we are concerned with in this book are the forms wherein this pattern may be expressed among men and women as defined by the most widespread and pervasive worldviews on the planet.

---

[11] I say possibly accompanying pleasure because it is quite possible to go through at least the first three stages of the pattern without experiencing the intense pleasure that can normally be expected. For example, wet dreams or in premature ejaculation there may be release without pleasure.

Variations in the Itch

There seems to be a wide variation in the presence of the itch and the frequency and methods of its release in the animal kingdom.

Frequency of the Itch

Lions reportedly copulate 20 to 50 times a day while other animals may do it once a year. A female fire ant mates once in a lifetime, while a female soay sheep has been observed copulating 163 times with 7 males in 5 hours.[12] The male praying mantis lives for his one and only sexual act when the female bites his head off when he is through.

Human males seem to get the itch anywhere from one to ten times a day, though the male sex has been reported, for example, to think about sex every three seconds. From my own observations, I have known men who have a relatively "low" sex drive and find that they need sexual release on an infrequent basis. On the other hand, I have known men and women who were irritable and frustrated if they didn't "have" sex three or more times a day. It appears that we are all unique in our drives and that there is no "normal" frequency. But whatever the cause, reason, or frequency of this itch, the fact is that it exists, it is and needs to be scratched in some way or another.

Variability in the Itch Object

In addition to variability in the frequency of the occurrence of the sexual itch in the animal kingdom, there is also variability in the object of the

---

[12] Soay sheep are miniature, primitive sheep found on the island of Hirta, St Kilda, the westernmost part of the British Isles. The event is cited in http://dannyre-views.com/h/Promiscuity.html.

ways in which the satisfaction of the itch is sought. Most people seem to gravitate to the man-and-woman variation, but there is also a significant minority that "naturally" seeks out either man-to-man or woman-to-woman contact. This is a natural variation, no matter what the centurions of the Catholic or any other faith may say about what is "natural."

There are also people who, for whatever the reason, are objectum sexuals, that is, seek out natural artifacts or objects as objects of sexual satisfaction. Similarly, there are those people whose objects are other natural animals. And then there are those who have been labeled with the pejorative term of sado-masochists who involve themselves in objects that are enslaved or brutalized in some way. Though I will not be considering these variations in the remainder of the book, they still need to be accounted for in a complete ethos of sexuality.

Satisfaction and Release

No matter what may be said to be the cause of, or reason for or extent of the sexual drive, all humans, of both sexes, have this drive for sexual release and satisfaction of some kind. All of us can relate to Mick Jagger's plaintive cry, "I can't get no satisfaction!" even if, like most people, he meant that he can't get any sex from a woman (presumably he could have, and maybe in this case **did** get some alternative form of satisfaction). Men, in particular, can relate to John F. Kennedy's father who is reported to have told him: "It's an itch that needs to be scratched," when JFK encountered him with one of his paramours—and certainly his sons and other descendents did nothing to discredit the notion.

All humans have this itch in some degree or another. Those who lose the drive for whatever reason can take the hormone testosterone (the male hormone, which governs the sexual drive in both men and women) to improve their desire and capacity for sex (defined as genital pleasure). The Internet is filled with numerous sites all offering various potions, ranging from Viagra to herbs and vitamins of various sorts that can improve the sexual drives for those people in whom it may be flagging or lacking.

In this book, I want to look at the ways in which the sexual itch may be relieved. I want to examine this issue from two points of view. First, I want to articulate a set of ideal types or forms that the release of sexual tensions may take. These types are logical and are developed on a logical basis independently of cultural norms.

Secondly, I want to look at the way a selected number of worldviews have dealt with the problem of how to relieve the sex drive and compare their views to the logical types of sexual expression. These worldviews seem to have placed some limit or other on ways in which the sexual itch can be scratched.[13] With that fact in mind, the six chapters following the next examine how six of the world's foremost worldviews—Buddhism, Christianity, Hinduism, Islam, Paganism and Taoism—include in or exclude from their views the logical forms of satisfaction from the itch.

---

[13] This book will not explore any of the biological or other reasons why these worldviews adopted one or another set of restrictions on sexual expression. If you are interested in how these restrictions arose, see Malcolm Pitts and Roger Short, *Ever Since Adam and Eve: The Evolution of Human Sexuality*, Cambridge University Press, 1999.

Chapter 1

Types of Sexual Expression

This chapter begins our exploration of sex by developing a typology of the logical forms of sexual expression. By logical forms, I mean something like what Max Weber meant by the notion of an ideal type, that is an abstract concept that can serve to characterize pure forms and can be used for the purposes of comparison and contrast.

There are six logically distinct forms of human sexual expression:

- Polymorph-amore
- Poly-amore
- Mono-amore
- Auto-amore
- Asexuality
- Non-sexuality

Note that these forms or ideal types of sexual expression are demarcated by the type of relationship that is involved and not on the sexual identity of the participants. This means that these forms of sexual expression could be found among men exclusively, among women exclusively, among men and women, and among people of either sex and some other being or object.

These types are arranged in a virtual inverted triangle that begins with the widest and most open attitude towards sexual expression then progressively restricts that expression until it no longer exists. The continuum when seen from top to bottom, begins with an "everything goes" view and ends with a "nothing goes" view.

Polymorph-amore—Many-to-Many

The first form that the release of sexual tensions may take is one that recognizes no limits on the forms the release may take and is open to release from all corners.

The first form of sexual relationship is one where there is a many-to-many relationship between the participants.[14] This form has several modes. One mode is the relationship between many men and many men, which is the norm in male gay experiences. Another mode is the relationship between many women and many women, which is less common in the female gay world. A third mode, more common throughout the world, is a relationship between many men and women to each other.

This is the view of sexual expression partly embodied in the "swinging" phenomenon that chugged through California at one time, before the advent of hosts of STIs (sexually transmitted infections) and AIDS. I say partly embodied because while bisexual women were more-or-less accepted in the swinging industry, the acceptance of bisexual men differed from swinging group to swinging group. Regardless, this was pleasure whenever it might be obtained, from men and women alike, particularly the women who had been liberated by contraceptive pills. No longer limited by the fears of conception or morality, swingers screwed their brains

---

[14] Polymorph-amore is a coined term, if you couldn't guess, that I am using here to distinguish the many-to-many from the one-to-many relationship which poly-amore covers. By polymorph-amore, I mean to indicate not only many loves of either sex, but many forms of love for both sexes.

out whenever they could, changing partners as easily and often as we change our food.

Communes, that invention of the Sixties, were also partially "swinging" communities in that group sex was encouraged, involving men with men, women with women, men with women, and men and women by themselves, though most communes soon evolved into "traditional" poly-amorous relationships, with the men having many women to please them (see Charles Manson).

This was heavenly. In fact, there is one major world religion, Islam, that conceives of heaven in precisely these terms: perpetual erections, girls who lose their virginity (Islamic men seem to like virginal girls) yet who revert immediately to virgins, and succulent young boys. Of course, even heaven seems to leave women and their pleasures out of the picture. Mohammed knew something, didn't he? If this is the heaven that awaits us after death, who wouldn't willingly die in any Jihad?

Writers in the sixties, like Norman O. Brown (in *Love's Body*) openly advocated and welcomed the new heaven on earth brought on by the sexual revolution in the West.[15] In that book, Brown refers to what we are calling polymorph-amore by the more judgmental term "polymorphous perversity."

Unhindered by responsibilities of raising children, making a living, or worrying about the possibilities of human extinction, surely this is the most universal and persistent vision of sexual expression. Do it, if it feels good. Perennial narcissism. Limitless sexuality. Men with women, men with men, women with women, people by themselves, people using dildos of various sorts, plastic dolls, bestiality (remember Deep Throat?). If it feels good, do it.

---

[15] See Norman O. Brown, *Love's Body*, University of California Press, 1990 (reissue of the 1966 edition).

Poly-amore—One-to-Many

Unlike the many-to-many form of sexual expression found in poly-morph-amore, where every woman and every man has many partners of both sexes as a constant diet, this second form of sexual expression, poly-amore, involves a limitation: it is one man to many women (polygyny), one women to many men (polyandry), one man with many men or one woman with many women (gays). While polygamy and its two subtypes (polygyny and polyandry) technically have to do with "marriage" relationships, I see no reason why it cannot be extended to include any form of sexual relationship involving a single person with multiple partners of the same or opposite sexes.[16] Homosexuality, whether of man-to-man or woman-to-woman types, may also be a form of polygamy (though there are obviously poly-morphous as well as monogamous homosexuals).

Polygyny—One man to Many Women

A polygynous form of sexual expression, in either married or unmarried modes, seems to be the norm throughout the world. African tribal chiefs and Islam practice polygyny (though it is generally called polygamy), as does a variant form of Mormonism, which was legal until 1862 when Lincoln outlawed but didn't exactly bend over backward to force Mormons to abide by the law. In Europe, where the norm is to like your wife and love your (current) mistress, this is also the norm. As much as he may like to think of himself as a real libertine, Hugh Hefner is strictly a one-man and many women kind of guy—a very ordinary polygynous lib-ertine and hardly a revolutionary.

---

[16] See http://www.scn.org/~spg, which is a Seattle-based web site for everything related to poly-amore.

Polyandry—One Woman to Many Men

Polyandry (one women with many men) is widely practiced through-out the world in the form of prostitution. There are also many individual women who have several simultaneous male lovers and are able to keep them all happy each day.

However, the anthropological literature mentions only two places where polyandry as a form of civil marriage is practiced (among the Nair people on the Malabar coast of India, and in parts of Tibet). The rarity of this form of marriage is probably due to the fact that polyandry is the primary form of relationship in Pagan societies where the Goddess is worshipped and where communal marriages predominate, that is in the hunter-gatherer stage of human evolution. Once we evolved into a sedentary life-style, patriarchal polygyny took over as the principal form of sexual relationship.

Mono-amore—One-to-One

The third major form of sexual relationship is one-to-one. As in the pre-vious form, this form has several modes that can be one man with one man, one woman with one woman, and, more commonly, one man with one woman.

A few animals, and most people throughout the world, express their sex-uality in one-to-one relationships, whether legal or extra-legal. For some people, the vital force of life, the élan vital, is naturally expressed through a longing of the one male for one female, one male for one male, or one female for one female. It is, rather, likely that this form of expression arises from fears, jealousies, selfishness, rather than any ontological need for one-to-one relating, but never mind that. Suffice it to say, that mono-amore is a universal—though, I venture to say—totally unsatisfying form of sexual expression. After the usual three months of passion, and especially after sev-eral years, one-on-one couples are reported to often be entirely without a sex life.

This form of sexual expression could also take the form of what has been called objectum sexuality, where there is a relationship between one person, man or woman, and some inanimate object, natural or spiritual (for example, god).

Mono-amore was prescribed in India, for example, only in 1955. In the West, the Roman law that allowed only one wife (but innumerable slave mistresses) was adopted throughout Christendom. Though enthroned in civil law, there is probably no reason for the rule beyond tradition (and possibly some religious or philosophical prejudice).

Auto-amore—One-on-One

A fourth form of sexual relationship is sex with oneself, one-on-one as distinct from one-to-one. As in previous forms, men by themselves or women by themselves may have a relationship of self-love.

In the technical literature, autoeroticism is identified with masturbation, and masturbation involves the stimulation of the genital organs to achieve orgasm. I am using the term auto-amore here instead of autoeroticism because I want to distinguish the form of sexuality I am interested in here (auto-amore) from masturbation. Certainly, all the previous forms of sexual expression described previously may involve masturbation, either by oneself or in mutual or group situations. So, auto-amore is not autoeroticism as technically understood.

As I am using the term auto-amore here, I am using it to mean a form of sexual expression that does not involve contact with other people in the flesh. It may involve various sexual aids, dildos and the like, pornography as aids to arousal, but it does not involve only masturbation (that is, while it may involve the stimulation of the genitals to achieve orgasm, it does not necessarily involve such stimulation, but may involve other forms of stimulation; for example, anal intercourse may result in orgasm without ever involving the penis) and it does not involve physical contact with other people (or other living beings, for that matter).

Hence, auto-amore as I am using it here is not just the primarily auto-erotic and narcissistic libido that Freud describes as existing prior to being directed outward to a love object (beyond the self). Auto-amore does have a sex object, namely another that is oneself.

Asexuality—One-to-None

The fifth form of sexual expression is negative sexuality or asexuality. In this form, the people involved, men or women, have the tools necessary for sexual expression but choose, voluntarily, to have no sexual expression of any kind.

This form of human sexual expression is one that has been enthroned by various religions (Buddhism and Christianity, for example) as the highest form of selfhood. It comes under various names, like abstinence and celibacy.

The key feature of this form of sexual expression is that it involves no sexual expression. The life force, the vital force, the semen or the egg, remain where they are; and the sexual urge is either sublimated or eliminated (or kept within). Lifelong and disciplined adherence to some yoga is required for this form of sexual expression, often with less than sterling success.

Non-sexuality

The final form of sexual expression is non-sexuality. This form is differentiated from asexuality by the fact that the people involved do not have the means for sexual expression.

For the majority of males born in the United States and Canada, it is still the practice of performing circumcision, which is a form of genital mutilation that does not, however, result in the eradication of the means of obtaining sexual pleasure.

However, when I speak of non-sexuality, I am thinking of eunuchs on the male side. At one time, these individuals presumably had the tools of sexual expression (sexual organs and drives), but were deprived of the tools (even if maybe not the drives) by having their sexual organs removed, oftentimes before the onset of puberty. The result is that such individuals cannot engage in sexual expressions.[17]

Similarly, on the female side we have a comparable form of non-sexuality, which is the result of women being subjected to genital mutilation. Genital mutilation is practiced in Africa, the Middle East (though it is not practiced by a majority of Muslims and there is nothing in the Quran about it) and elsewhere throughout the world, including North and South America, Asia, and Europe. It is estimated that currently 135 million women in the world have been mutilated.[18]

Though genital mutilation may be a form of objectum sexuality and could be placed under some other category, it is clear that it is practiced in strongly patriarchal societies where men do this to deprive the women of the pleasures of sex and also the desire while retaining the capacity for sex with men, and, of course, procreation.

Organization of Religion Chapters

The six worldviews selected for description in this book were chosen because all of them fit into a continuum ranging from the least to the most restrictive views of sexual expression. Beginning with Paganism, which is the least restrictive and most open view to all types of sexual expression, the range of worldviews ends with Buddhism, which may be considered the most restrictive inasmuch as from its perspective all material or sensual features of existence are illusion and should be avoided.

---

[17] See http://www.eunuch.org/index2.php for an interesting description of the phenomenon of eunuchs. One interesting fact pointed out here is that because sexual expression was lacking in their lives, many eunuchs became gourmands.

[18] See http://www.amnesty.org/ailib/intcam/femgen/fgm1.htm#a5.

Between these two extremes, we find Taoism, then Islam, Hinduism and Christianity, which are each successively more restrictive than is Paganism. So, you will find the worldviews described in the following order:

- Paganism—**All** forms of sexual expression are natural and good.
- Taoism—**Most** forms of sexual expression are natural and healthy.
- Islam—**Few** forms of sexual expression (mono-amore and polygyny) are all right.
- Hinduism—**One** form of sexual expression, mono-amore, is all right.
- Christianity—**No** form of sexual expression is good. If you must, choose mono-amore.
- Buddhism—**No** form of desire is all right. If you must, choose mono-amore.

Chapter 2

Paganism

The theme of Paganism is that all forms of sexual expression are natural and tolerated.

Paganism is the worldview that guided humans for 99 percent of their existence. Only in the last 10,000 years or so have we adopted worldviews other than Pagan. Paganism is a naturalistic worldview with an open and tolerant attitude towards sexual expression.

What is Paganism?

We should note at the start that I am using Paganism[19], perhaps in an atypical sense, to refer generically to the whole host of so-called primitive, polytheistic religions that preceded all the other (documented) organized worldviews and that continue to exist today in a variety of forms. For example, when asked to characterize the religious beliefs of Haitians, it is

---

[19] Please note that I am capitalizing Paganism, Pagan and other terms because the worldview has as much right to being a noun as do Christianity or Islam or any other worldview.

common for people there to assert: "They are 60 percent Catholic, 40 percent Protestant, and 100 percent Voodoo."[20]

My view is that this is probably true globally. A country may be nominally Catholic or Protestant, for example, Nigeria or Kenya, but it is also in all likelihood 100 percent supportive of the local, indigenous religions. The Pagan religion or world-view, the folk religion, certainly underlies the belief systems of all of southern Africa, most of Asia, all of Latin America south of the Mexican border (and much above it!), and wherever shamanistic or other indigenous belief systems predominate.

In all parts of the world, we find such Pagan religions existing side-by-side with or as an underground movement. England has its Druids; America has its native American worldviews; Australia has its Aborigines; New Zealand has its Maoris; Haiti has its Vodun (as Voodoo is most properly referred to); and Cuba has its Santeria.

The Pagan worldview is the worldview that predominated for 99 percent of human existence. Before the rise of a sedentary, agriculturally based life that began only 10,000 years ago or so, we were hunter-gatherers. Our lives were communally based and we hunted and gathered our food from what nature provided. There was no private property and the group or the tribe as a whole owned whatever was owned. This was the time when the "Great Mother" was the main object of adoration. Then we started agriculture and patriarchy, private ownership, and sexual restrictions of various sorts began to be placed on our heretofore-unrestricted behavior.

Pagan religions have existed at least since the oldest times and are the oldest form of worldview known to us. It is also the most widespread worldview, for adherents are found on all continents. All of the organized religions are derived from Paganism, either as a development or as a refinement or departure from it.[21] While all mainline worldviews such as those

---

[20] I grew up in Haiti, if you're wondering.

[21] See, for example, *The Jesus Mysteries: Was the Original Jesus a Pagan God*, by Timothy Freke and Peter Gandy, New York: Harper Collins, 1999.

already mentioned and including Communism, Taoism, Hinduism, Buddhism, and others, may claim adherents throughout the world, my guess is that the world's leading worldview is Paganism pure and simple.

The term, Pagan, which is Latin for peasant, was originally used by the Roman Christian sect thousands of years ago to refer to all people who did not accept the monotheistic theology of Christianity.[22] As such, it was originally a term of condemnation and remains so when used by Christians to this day. In the late twentieth century, however, the term is used in an honorific sense to refer to all religions that honor most or all of the basic tenets of the polytheistic worldviews.

While Paganism may be the global folk religion, in our day the term Neo-paganism is used to refer to those religions that mimic in some degree the basic tenets of the Pagan religions and seek to live in accordance with them. Among the Neo-pagan religions are to be found such folkways as Druidism, Voodooism, and Wicca.

Unlike the more formal established or organized religions, which have their own book (for example the Jewish Torah, the Quran of Islam, or the writings of the disciples of Buddha), Paganism has no book, no organized set of doctrines or beliefs, and no fixed revelation. If they have a book at all, it is the book of nature. The best that can be done, therefore, is to characterize the attitudes and behavioral presuppositions of the worldview since there are so many variations in Paganism and nothing that can quite be called a belief, in the sense of a proposition that expresses the faith thereof. In what follows, therefore, I will attempt to characterize the attitudes rather than the beliefs of Pagans.[23]

---

[22] Included among the Pagans are such luminaries as Socrates, Plato, and Aristotle.

[23] Only those worldviews that have been written down and codified can be said to have beliefs that can be stated as proposition such as "I believe in the triune God…" Since Paganism is a pre-literate world-view most often characterized in stories in an oral tradition, even if these traditions have been written down, it is best to characterize their worldviews as attitudes or behavioral presuppositions rather than beliefs.

Naturalism

I want to begin with what could be called the basic principle of the Pagan worldview insofar as the nature of reality is concerned because their ontological principle contrasts sharply with the ontological principles of the world's other major worldviews.

The cardinal feature of Paganism is that it is naturalistic. Reality, whatever it may be, is through and through natural and whole. There is no spiritual realm that stands in distinction to a so-called natural realm. Reality is nature and nature is reality. Nature is that out of which we appear and that to which we return.

The most immediate and obvious reality of nature is the earth. Pagans feel that nature is divine and as such are strong environmentalists. They celebrate cycles of the sun and moon and often worship outdoors. Some do so in the nude. They also believe that all plants and animals in the world are equal and will often say a prayer of thanks before doing something as simple as pulling a vegetable out of a garden. All Pagans celebrate the cycles of nature like the seasons and build their rituals around these natural cycles. All Paganisms honor wilderness over the humanized parts of nature.

Animism

A second major feature of Paganism is that nature is seen as filled with life. Earth itself is not an alien presence, but a living being. While dressed up in scientific jargon, the so-called Gaia hypothesis of James Lovelock, which regards earth as alive (mother earth), is a Neo-pagan rejuvenation of an ancient Pagan idea.[24] But not only is the earth as a whole, that is our most proximate experience of nature alive, but so are all of its other parts. Not only are they alive, but also deities, spirits, govern them. Everything has a soul, or anima or spirit. This includes animals, plants, rocks, mountains, rivers, stars, in fact any existent whatsoever. Each anima is powerful and so can help or hurt people, including the souls of the dead or the ancestors.[25]

Thus, we find in Paganism a plethora of gods or divinities. There are water gods and village gods, and seasonal gods and gods of every shape and description, each one watching over or governing various aspects of our lives.

There is also a strong tradition within Paganism to think that there is an overarching "great spirit". This is not monotheism, which holds that there is only one divinity, but a sort of super deity among a plethora of divinities.

Pluralism

The multiplicity of natural divinities points to another of the key features of Paganism, namely its pluralism. Pagans are polytheistic in believing in many gods or divinities, but they are also pluralistic in holding that there are many ways to live just as there are many divinities to interact with. This is something it shares with Hinduism.

---

[24] See http://www.magna.com.au/~prfbrown/gaia.html. This page discusses the hypothesis initially presented by Lovelock and subsequently given extensive scientific support by Lynn Margulis.

[25] The Bible of Christians condemn Pagans with very strong words, saying they are "abominations to God", and urging the good Christians to "stone them to death" (Deut.18, Lev.20, Isa.44,47, Mat.10). The Quran of Islam is equally harsh.

This pluralism stands in sharp contrast to the dominant dualisms of the organized religions, and particularly Christianity with its sharp dualism between good and evil, right and wrong, heaven and hell, the right way and the wrong way. Of course, the three major monotheisms are alike in this regard, for they hold that their god is the only god and the others are false gods. For Pagans, on the other hand, your god is as good as and no better than my god—and all ways are equally valid, provided, of course, that they do not attempt to prescribe what other people may believe (which is impossible for the monotheisms to do because they are non-pluralistic by nature).

Anti-Authoritarian

Authoritarianism is a product of any view that holds that there can and ought to be a single, centralized control center for every human action or form of behavior. From the fact of its polytheism and pluralism, we may infer that Pagans do not accept any authority in matters of life and morals. There are as many ways as there are people.

In addition, since the aim of life is to fit into the patterns and cycles of nature rather than to dominate and control nature, authority is rejected. Each individual is his own authority. In many ways, Pagans are the original libertarians. For Pagans, there is no closeted priesthood. In Wicca, the most widely known Pagan worldview today, for example, anyone of either sex can become a Witch (as priests or priestesses are known).

Sexuality

The preceding description of the attitudes of Pagans gives us an idea of what their views about sexuality and sexual expression would be.

First, we are all part of nature and whatever exists is natural and good. The sexual itch exists, it is part of nature, part of life, and it is infused with divinity just like everything else. If everything physical is also simultaneously spiritual, it follows that everything natural is good and there is no sin or restriction except natural ones. Sex is (as among the animals) a perfectly necessary, instinctive and unselfconscious activity. It is harmonious with itself, natural, and unproductive of evil.

The largest group within Neo-paganism is the Wiccans. Rather than viewing human sexuality as separate and often antagonistic to religion, many Wiccans integrate sexuality, faith and practice. The Council of American Witches issued a statement about their religion during their Spring Witchmeet of 1974, held in Minneapolis, MN. It says, in part: "We value sexuality as pleasure, as the symbol and embodiment of Life, and as one of the sources of energies used in magickal practices and religious worship."[26]

Wiccans regard human sexuality as a gift of the Goddess and God. It is an activity to be enjoyed in accordance with the Wiccan Rede. One form of the Rede is: "Do what you wish, as long as it harms no one, including yourself."[27]

The "Charge of the Goddess" is an instruction of unknown antiquity that is recognized by many Neo-pagans. One part of it reads: "All acts of pleasure are my rituals."[28] Some Wiccans engage in the Great Rite, which includes sexual intercourse in private between a committed couple as part of a circle religious ritual. I suspect that masturbation by solitary practitioners also forms part of some one-person Wiccan rituals.[29]

Since Pagans tend to celebrate life in all of its aspects, honoring wildness, and following and celebrating the natural rhythms of life and nature, the sexual itch would not be seen as a problem with restrictions and injunctions of all sorts, as we find in the major religions, but something to

---

[26] See the "Principles of Wiccan Belief" at http://www.wrcf.org/acw.htm.

[27] See http://wicca.drak.net/proteus/rede.htm.

[28] There are numerous versions of the Charge available on the Internet. See, for example, http://www.bungalow.com/charge.html.

[29] See http://www.witchvox.com/xgay.html.

be celebrated. Just as you eat when you are hungry, so you should relieve yourself of the itch when it occurs. Christians, who are notorious body haters and admirers of restraint and abstinence, would regard the natural attitudes of Pagans to sex as animalistic—and, of course, Pagan.[30]

Since there is no reason to withhold oneself from extinguishing the irritations of the sexual itch, sex at any time and place is acceptable. Since there are numerous divinities that may appear at any time and place in nature, among them the sexual desire, there are numerous ways of placating the divinity.

There is no inherent reason among Pagans to restrict the forms of sexual expression. If one is inclined to auto-amore, then that is fine; if one is inclined to mono-amore, then that is fine; if one is inclined to poly-amore, then that too is fine. Whatever way the plurality of humans with their plurality of divinities, find to celebrate the sexual instinct is fine. The only rule, if it may so be termed, is "Do no harm, but do whatever thou wilt."[31] Celibacy and abstinence, on the other hand, may serve some purpose as some specific time, but as general attitudes, they are probably unhealthy and, yes, unnatural. Similarly, the genital mutilation of men, for other than criminal offenses, is not practiced, nor is the genital mutilation of women.

Food, drink, sex. These are natural and good. Enjoying oneself, having fun, or feeling good are natural and life-affirming events. All of these are natural and acceptable. Pagans tend to love celebrations, love celebrating

---

[30.]As Walter Wakefield and Austin Evans in their *Heresies of the High Middle Ages*, Columbia University Press, New York, 1991, describe in great detail, there were many Christian heresies that came close to Pagan beliefs. For example, the heresy of the Free Spirit, whose followers believed in doing whatever felt good (the original hippies?).

[31.]This is a cardinal principle among the followers of the modern Pagan worldview known as Wicca. Note that the great St. Augustine is reported to have said something quite similar, "Love God, and do what you will."

nature, and don't have the hang-ups that people have who developed within the worldview of the Christian west. Sex exists, sex is fun, it is pleasurable, and it is definitely OK. If it feels good, do it.

Summary

From the foregoing, we get an understanding of the Pagan conception of sexual expression, which is as follows:

- OK to Celibacy (abstaining from sex) if that's what you want
- Yes to Auto-amore if that's what you want
- Yes to Poly-amore
- OK to Polygyny
- OK to Polyandry
- OK to Mono-amore
- Non-sexuality is abnormal and unnatural

In this view, then, the full range of the sexual forms are acceptable forms of behavior and are not proscribed in any way though some forms (such as auto-amore, asexuality or non-sexuality) may be regarded as unnatural and perverse—but not proscribed.

Chapter 3

Taoism

The theme of Taoism is that most but not all forms of sexual expression are natural and healthy.

While not as open as Paganism, Taoism is more closely related to the naturalism of Paganism than it is to the other worldviews.

What is Taoism?

Tao means the way or the path. The way or path in question is the one articulated in a short, two-day book allegedly written by Lao-Tse[32] (604-531 BCE), a contemporary of Confucius, based on the harmony of yin and yang, the polar opposites that characterize the world. This view is stated succinctly in Verse 42[33]:

---

[32] Some scholars claim that there was no such person, but that instead the book was compiled over several hundred years by a number of anonymous writers.

[33.]See http://members.home.net/mayoi/ly-ttc.htm for a translation by Lin Yutang. There are around a hundred translations, no two of them alike.

Out of Tao, One is born;

Out of One, Two;

Out of Two, Three;

Out of Three, the created universe.

The created universe carries the yin at its back

and the yang in front;

Through the union of the pervading principles it

reaches harmony.

Central here is the notion that everything is an indivisible whole operating according to the fundamental laws, which are expressed as the unity of the opposites, yin and yang. Everything that is manifested in the world has these two polar opposites—in everything, there is yin and yang, female and male, reception and creation, passivity and activity. We need to understand and harmonize our lives with these laws (and thus with the Tao) if we are to live a good life.

What we know of today as Taoism in fact developed from the confluence of three different rivers (and innumerable schools). One tributary was the philosophy articulated in the *I Ching*. Another was the aphoristic tradition exemplified by the above passage from the *Tao Te Ching*. The third contributory stream was the alchemical tradition with numerous schools that represented the "Tantric" leanings of the Taoists.[34] This latter river has a tradition known as Shaktism that interprets some sayings of Lao-Tse as indicating that he was a worshipper of the vulva (yoni puta). Another rivulet is devoted to health and longevity and emphasizes sperm retention. It is this latter school that will be used as a basis for the interpretation of sexual expression provided here.

---

[34] The classic text for this tradition is the so-called Dragon-Tiger. See Eva Wong's translation and commentary in *Harmonizing Yin an Yang*, Boston: Shambala, 1997.

The Taoist ideas began really as a psychology or philosophy and evolved into a worldview. In 440 BCE, it was adopted as the Chinese state religion, something it shared with Confucianism, and stayed that way until 1911 when state support for the religion (or worldview) was withdrawn. When the communists took over in China, they rejected Taoism for its passivity, fatalism, and submissive ethics.

While the philosophy itself along with Confucianism may no longer hold official sanction in China, both still pervade the Chinese ethos. While Confucius may be the guru of social and political life, the Tao is the guru of the natural and harmonious life. While Taoism is a matriarchal view, Confucianism is a patriarchal view. In modern political language, while Taoism is individualistic and libertarian, Confucius is conservative and collectivistic in its emphasis on tradition and propriety.[35] Since our lives are woven from these two strands, there is no real need to choose between them, and this is so in China where one can be both Confucian (or now Marxist and Capitalist) in social life and Taoist in private life.

Classical Taoism was a reinterpretation of traditional nature worship and divination. In other words, Taoism is a rationalized Paganism. While the Tao (or Dao) is an indivisible force or power that pervades the universe, it manifests itself in all that exists, so Taoism recognizes that spirits pervade nature and manifest the Tao. Taoism is still a naturalistic worldview like Paganism, but it is one that is rationalized by the abstract principles of yin and yang and their complex interactions. Since yin is identified with the female and yang with the male—which is, in my opinion a mistake—the forms of sexual behavior seem also to be limited primarily to the pairing of males and females.

---

[35] Confucianism supposedly resulted in some 3300 rules of social conduct, while Lao-Tse's poem can be read in quite a few places as a scathing critique of the use of laws and rules to coerce human behavior.

The view of Taoism and sexuality to be presented here is derived from Tantric Taoism, that is from associated studies and not directly from the Taoist teachings.[36] Since the aim of the path is to learn to live in harmony with the opposites, in sexual matters the aim is to learn to bring men and women into a balance. We can articulate what this means best by considering the various forms of sexual expression.

Polymorph-amore

In the normal, it is quite apparent that men and women are quite different and out of kilter. In the natural state of things, women are supreme where sex and procreation are concerned. Before the development of an agricultural mode of life, when men took over as the "superior" sex, women were the masters. Matriarchy, which existed in pre-agricultural times, recognized this. Women had complete sexual freedom and were often unable to control their sex drives. Descent was traced through women. Women "had" as many (or few) men as they wanted. In the natural state of things, women were the good—and men being little more than the seed-bearers of the next generation.

In the state of nature, before the development of settled agriculture, there was a natural balance between men and women. Women were the insatiable sex and all men in the collective were available to them. However, when agriculture and a settled way of existence came upon the scene an imbalance resulted. Women were limited to a single man so descendents could be identified and property transfers to descendents made. However, an imbalance between the sexes resulted because of the

---

[36] There are numerous books on the tao of something or other. The following books could profitably be used as an introduction to the subject of Taoism and sex. See Daniel P. Reid, *The Tao of Health, Sex and Longevity*, New York: Simon and Schuster, 1989; and Stephen T. Chang, *The Tao of Sexology*, New York: Tao Publishing, 1986.

differences between men and women in their sexual natures. To achieve a state of harmony between men and women in an agricultural setting requires a change in the basic behavior of men—though not of women. To understand the change in behavior that needs to occur, we need to understand the sexual differences between men and women.

Women and men differ sexually basically in their orgasms. Women retain their fluids when orgasm occurs, while men lose their fluids, thus exhausting themselves. When a man has ejaculated, he is essentially through and ready to fall asleep, while women remain ever able and willing for more sex. In order to give women what they need, men have to learn to practice sex in such a way that a single man can still satisfy a woman the way she was satisfied by the multiple couplings that she enjoyed in the state of nature, before agriculture.

The key to this sexual practice is for men to restrict their ejaculations. The method of ejaculation restriction gives men an ability to enjoy sex with women as much as they want and this results in a harmony between men and women in an agricultural or settled existence. By restricting their ejaculations, men are able to engage in multiple couplings throughout a day and do not just fall asleep after sex.

Poly-amore

The Taoist emphasis is not on the number of partners so much as on the type of sex involved. Good sex is not a matter of feeling or affection, but of technique. And the technique is restricted ejaculation.

One woman with many men is all right in a state of nature. It is all right when in a settled life provided that the men practice healthy sex, otherwise this is just sex that benefits the women only.

Homosexuality among women is also all right because women preserve their fluids and lesbian sex is healthy for them. The more such same-sex couplings women have, the better. Two women together means that there are two passive (yin) principles together and this is all right.

For men, however, homosexuality is another matter. Whether it's one man to one man or many men together, homosexuality is unhealthy in principle because when men ejaculate, they lose zinc and a fluid that is twenty percent cerebrospinal fluid. Ejaculation thus depletes men of their vitality. In addition, two men together means that there are two aggressive (yang) principles together, which result in conflict. This conflict is psychological in that the two aggressive principles fight with each other and one man ends up playing a passive (and unnatural) role. The conflict is also physiological, causing weakness and fatigue.[37]

Mono-amore

Healthy sex is sex of a certain type between men and women. In a state of nature, polyandry (one women and many men) is natural and good. When we move to a settled, agricultural existence, however, one man and one woman is best—but only if the man practices restricted ejaculation.

The reason for this is that when men practice the unhealthy habit of ejaculation every time they have sex, they inevitably lean toward polygyny (one man and many women), yet it is impossible for any one man to satisfy one woman much less many women. Since women are insatiable sexually, the best that man can do in a settled existence is to have one woman with whom they have sex, and to practice the art of restricted ejaculation. If men do want multiple partners, that is all right so long as they practice this art with all their women, though psychologically it's probably best to settle for one partner at a time, or well-known partners if one is interested in having multiple sex partners.

---

[37] I think that the identification of yin with females and yang with males is mistaken. As we know today, each man or woman shares in so-called male and female tendencies, with men about 55 percent male and 45 percent female, and women 55 percent female and 45 percent male.

Auto-amore

Auto-amore and one of its prime modes of expression, masturbation, differ by gender.

Women may masturbate forever, endlessly, since their sexual fluids are retained within their bodies to nourish them. When women are deprived of the companionship of men, masturbation and homosexuality are OK and should be encouraged.

For men, on the other hand, masturbation and homosexuality are unhealthy habits. Auto-amore masturbation among men is all right when men are young, from teens to twenty-one, but after that masturbation starts to cause weakness in the thighs and knees, the loss of vitality, and general depression. After the age of thirty, men should stop masturbation altogether and save their semen for sharing with women. If they practice restricted ejaculation, they should also ejaculate only around once or twice a month at the most, and much less than that after reaching the age of sixty.

Asexuality

A key to the Taoism view of sexuality is that there is a difference between healthy and unhealthy sex. Unhealthy sex is sex that causes degeneration and unhealthiness, while healthy sex provides well-being.

One of the things that contribute to health are the hormones of various kinds that are produced during sex. If we fail to produce these hormones, we open ourselves, both men and women, to diseases and degeneration.

Hence, celibacy is not a healthy mode of sexual expression since it deprives men and women of sexual stimulation. Celibacy will cause illnesses and ill health as much as indulgence will. Vows of celibacy to the contrary, nothing will stop the energy of sexuality and if this energy is not used properly it will affect the life and health of the person involved.

Non-Sexuality

While the Chinese are known to practice female infanticide, effectively mutilating the lives of women at birth, there is virtually no known practice of female genital mutilation. Similarly, there is no tradition of developing eunuchs from male genital mutilation, so non-sexuality is not a known practice in China.

Summary

From the foregoing, we get an understanding of the Taoist conception of sexual expression, which is as follows:

- No to Celibacy
- Yes to Auto-amore, but only when practicing restricted ejaculation
- Yes to Poly-amore, but only when practicing restricted ejaculation
- No to Polygyny
- OK to Polyandry
- OK to Mono-amore
- Non-sexuality is abnormal and unnatural

In this view, then, the full range of the sexual forms with some exceptions are acceptable forms of behavior and are not proscribed in any way, though some forms (such as auto-amore, asexuality or non-sexuality) may be regarded as unhealthy.

Chapter 4

Islam

The theme of Islam is that a few forms of sexual expression (mono-amore and polygyny) are acceptable. While Islam does recognize the "fires" of sexuality, it is not a natural view like either Paganism or Taoism, but is a much more restrictive view of sexuality. On the other hand, Islam isn't as restrictive as are Hinduism, Christianity or Buddhism.[38]

What is Islam?

It is common in the West to claim that Islam is the latest of the three major monotheisms that have arisen in the world, the other two being Judaism and Christianity. In this view, Mohammed proclaimed a new religion in Arabia as an alternative to Judaism and Christianity. However,

---

[38] We should note at the start that Islamic law and theology are closely intertwined; there is no church-state separation as in known in the US. Islamic law, known as the Shari's is based on the Quran, the Sunna (discussions between Mohammed and his closest disciples), and Ijma (consensus opinions of scholars). My interpretation of the Islamic views on sex, however, relies mainly on the Quran.

For the most part, references are to the Quran (by chapter and verse, as in 1:1).

a reading of the Quran shows that Mohammed considered himself and is considered as a prophet who tried to recall his people to the "original" religion of Abraham. Instead of enunciating a new religion, he was a "fundamentalist" who felt that Judaism and Christianity had betrayed the monotheism of Abraham and his duty was to call the people—including Jews and Christians—back to the original monotheism. From the standpoint of Islam, then, Islam is not a new religion, not a third monotheism but the original, real monotheism that existed before it was perverted by the Jews and Christians.

Whether regarded as a third monotheism or as the foundational monotheism out of which Judaism and Christianity arose, Islam is a religion of contradictions. At some points, the Quran suggests that Islam should respect the religion of other peoples, yet at other places it suggests that a true Muslim has a duty to wage war (Jihad) against all non-believers, up to and including putting them to death. Similarly, Islam rails vehemently against all polytheism and idolatry, yet some of its practitioners, notably the kings, emirs, and aristocrats are notorious for their many wives and numerous offspring. Similarly, while it proclaims a god, Allah, who is without gender and created men and women to be equal, many of those who follow the religion are, to put it diplomatically, women haters.

As far as sexuality is concerned, the Prophet recognizes the raging fires of the libido, but sought to quench these fires through a polygynist strategy—while it would be better, he said, to stick to one wife, anyone can have up to four at one time and also have temporary marriages (such as one finds in relationships between men and prostitutes).

Polymorph-amore

One of the reasons that Mohammed saw as the need to recall people to the Islamic religion[39] is that in the "days of ignorance" (that is, in a pre-

---

[39] It is not correct to see the Prophet as the originator of Islam. Rather, he is regarded as the last prophet of a pre-existing religion whose origin was with Abraham (the Jewish patriarch).

Islamic state) people were totally consumed by their desires and lusts. Illicit relationships and other types of immorality were common among the mostly unregenerate and unenlightened tribal populace.

Since Islam is a reaction against the anarchy and disorder (mental, medical, and economic) brought about by conflicting tribal allegiances and unbridled sexual license, polymorph-amore is an unacceptable mode of sexual expression for Muslims.

Throughout the Quran, the Prophet makes frequent references to three types of pre-Islamic behavior systems that Allah abhors. One is to monkeys. Apes, the Quran says, are despicable (7:166); they engage in acts that are unacceptable. Since we know that chimpanzees (that are 98% genetically like us) are known to engage in what we would call promiscuous behavior, where the female in estrus makes herself available to all males, and males and females are known to engage in homosexual behavior, we can guess that this is partly what the Quran is referring to.

The Quran also makes frequent references to despicable behaviors that arise out of "polytheism" and "idolatry" (98:1), two belief systems that are common to pre-monotheistic cultures and which existed in the Arabia of his day, where sexual license was also generally prevalent.[40]

On the other hand, what the Prophet takes away with one hand he returns with the other. In his descriptions of paradise, we are given an image of unbridled sensuality and the fulfillment of all desires (see, for example, 76:13): Therein there shall be rivers of water, the taste and smell of which are never changed; rivers of milk the taste of which will remain unchanged; rivers of wine that will be delicious to those who drink from it and rivers of clear, pure honey.

---

[40] Prior to the promulgation of Islam, Mecca was host to idols representing the myriad of tribal gods that were dominant at the time.

Dressed in silk, believers will recline on thrones of gold, surrounded by ever-young girls and ever-young boys ready to serve their every wish and to bring them delight. Never-ending erections; eternal orgasms; every sensual delight imaginable—nothing is denied to them.

So, maybe it is only on earth that polymorph-amore is a problem—once we get to heaven, it will be the norm and the wish of Allah. The Prophet sure had a good thing going, didn't he?

Poly-amore

The basic metaphysical unit in Islam is the pair (36:36, Allah "created in pairs all things…"), specifically the pair of man and woman. Men and women were created from a "single soul" (4:1) and are meant for each other. Hence, the form of relationship required of humans is marriage, where pairs meet—meet, but do not become one as in Christianity.[41]

In one aspect, marriage is an act pleasing to Allah because it is in accordance with his[42] commandments that husband and wife love each other and help each other to continue the human race and rear and nurse their children to become true servants of Allah.

In another aspect, marriage is a lawful response to the basic biological instinct to have sexual intercourse and to procreate children, so the Islamic system of laws has prescribed detailed rules for translating this response into a living human institution reinforced by a whole framework of legally

---

[41] Islam does not require that "two become one" as Christianity requires of its marriages. Rather, men and women retain their identities and separate interests. Women's kingdom is the home; men's kingdom is the public world.

[42] Though Allah is referred to as "he" this does not imply that Allah is a male for he is totally beyond gender differentiation. This may account for the reason why Islam gives women, at least in theory, many rights equal to men. Islamic society is thus in many ways both patriarchal and matriarchal.

enforceable rights and duties, not only of the spouses, but also of their off-spring.

"When a man marries, he has fulfilled half of his religion, so let him fear Allah regarding the remaining half," says the Prophet. The Prophet considered marriage for a Muslim as half of his religion because it shields him from promiscuity, adultery, fornication, homosexuality etc., which ultimately lead to many other evils like slander, quarreling, homicide, loss of property and disintegration of the family.

Though mono-amore is probably the norm in Islam, an acceptable form of sexual relations is the form of polygynous marriage. Polygyny is legally and theologically acceptable. The Quran states that a man may have two, three, or four wives (4:3), possibly more, so long as he can "deal justly" with them all (which means not only providing for them in the same house as himself, but also being able to give them the gift of his semen on a regular basis)—otherwise, have only one wife.

As we know, Mohammed himself had ten wives (some traditions say thirteen)[43], and many a king or emir in Islamic countries has been known to have hundreds (for example, Saudi kings have had hundreds of wives, maybe just four at a time), which accounts for the ten thousand or more "princes" and princesses in the kingdom today) or thousands of wives (the Emir of Kuwait who seemed anxious to follow in the footsteps of King Solomon). Nevertheless, most Muslims have only one wife either because they cannot afford more or because they agree with Mohammed's point that no matter how hard they try no man can deal equitably with more

---

[43] While this fact has been taken as a sign of Mohammed's lustfulness, the facts are that he married a 40-year old woman when he was 25 and was faithful to her for 24 years. His plural marriages occurred late in his life and several of his wives were the wives of fallen comrades. The reasons for his support of polygamy probably had less to do with lust than with a sense of responsibility for widows. However, see

http://www.light-of-life.com/eng/reveal/r5405et7.htm#p123.

than one wife (4:129). A woman cannot prevent her husband from taking another wife, but she has the legal right to divorce him if he does.

Normal Polygynous Marriage

Islam considers sexuality an absolutely normal and natural urge of every human being. Symbolic of this positive attitude is the important place sex is accorded in paradise.

Islamic representations of paradise depict a height of delights, with, among other things, girls whose virginity is continually renewed, immortal boys as beautiful as hidden pearls, perpetual erections and infinite orgasms.

On earth, however, because of human imperfection, sex has a problematic side, which makes regulation necessary. Unregulated sex threatens the social order and leads to anarchy and chaos, and therefore has to be restricted to marriage. Social order and the God-given harmony of life are threatened by the suppression of sexuality in celibacy and by sexual acts outside of marriage, heterosexual as well as homosexual.

Sexual activity outside of marriage is adultery and is condemned (4:15) and women who engage in it may be stoned, as they still are under the Taliban in Afghanistan and in Iran. Fewer, if any, men seem to fall into adultery, either because the rules of marriage (and divorce) are so loose or because it is "expected" of them.

Temporary Marriages

In addition to allowing a man to have multiple wives concurrently, the Prophet also created another institution, that of "temporary" marriages (mutia), whereby those people who did not have a current wife or found themselves in a foreign country or just couldn't control their sexual urges (and couldn't afford to get married) could arrange a "temporary" marriage, with the same rights and responsibilities as a real marriage—except that it would be of a shorter duration. Thus, the Emir of Kuwait has made just about every woman in his emirate a "queen for a day". This is surely another convenient way to give men a way to cope with their lusts. The Ayatollah Khomeni, a noted misogynist, used this concept to justify prostitution, which is rampant in Iran.

Poly-amore in Islam

The end result of the Islamic view is thus that (1) the sex urge exists; (2) its proper expression is through pairing of men and women in marriage; (3) men being the aggressive sex may have up to four or more wives concurrently (if the marriage agreement specifies it), and may upon occasion have "temporary" wives. Polyandry (one wife with many husbands) is not even considered; it is a form of illicit sexuality and certainly violates the law that men are protectors and maintainers of women because they are stronger (4:34), for polyandry would give women a "superior" place.

Homosexual poly-amore is condemned. Homosexuality is considered adultery (4:16), in part, though sodomy in any form is condemned (29:28-29), and Islamic law sees it as a crime against humanity, which opens the door to many other shameful acts, and affects the reputation and property of the family, thereby disrupting the social fabric.[44]

So, that leaves only polygyny[45] as a legitimate form of poly-amore.

---

[44] In a story widely circulated on November 14, 2001, an Egyptian court convicted several homosexual men for debauchery and "the defamation of manhood." Also see http://www.islamic.org.uk/homosex.html for a discussion of the Islamic view of homosexuality.

[45] Actually, biologically it is to the genetic interest of men to have as many women as possible, while for the female it is better to have but one man. Geneticists will confirm this.

Mono-amore

If and only if the man does not have the desire or means to have multiple wives and the first and subsequent wives agree does mono-amore have any legal or ethical import. Hence, mono-amore is an acceptable, but not normative form of sexual expression. Mono-amore may also be the wisest course of action for a man whose wife will not agree to more wives, or a man who wishes to be able to keep a lustful wife satisfied, or one who wants to maintain peace and tranquility in the home, all reasonable considerations as far as the Quran is concerned.

Since homosexuality is not an acceptable form of relationship, even mono-amore of man-to-man is not acceptable.

Auto-amore

Since the natural and normal—and god-required—form of sexual expression is between men and women and since the purpose of women is to give men a way to have (legitimate) sex (2:187), we may assume that the Prophet would also reject auto-amore. Since fornication is forbidden (4:24) and adultery between men (i.e., homosexuality) is forbidden (26:165), we may assume that any form of sexual release that does not involve a woman and is not in a "marriage" relationship is forbidden, considered an evil, and certainly, if carried on exclusively does not result in procreation, which is one of the guarantees of Islam.

In addition, since Islam is one of the three religions that descended from Abraham, and since Islam regards parts of the Jewish bible and parts of the Christian bible as forming part of the Islamic revelation (which culminated in the Prophet), we may assume that the views of auto-eroticism in the Jewish and Christian traditions would be shared by Islam.[46]

---

[46] Though there are historical reasons why Judaism and Christianity do not condone polygamy, polygyny was common among Jews at one time (the most famous being Solomon with his 700 wives and 300 concubines, and also King David), and there is no restriction in the Jewish part of the Bible against polygamy.

Asexuality—Celibacy and Abstinence

Islam is a realistic and practical religion. Whatever else may be said about the Islamic view of sexuality, Islam clearly recognizes that the sexual instinct is a fact of life. The Prophet (Mohammed) speaks often of the need to find ways to "quench the fires" of the sex instinct. About the fact of these sexual drives, Islam has a very realistic view: there is no denying that they exist; there is, equally, no denying that ways must be found to satisfy these drives.

While the Prophet saw the religion as a way of canalizing and humanizing the sexual urges, it does not ignore nature in this search. It does not advocate ways of quenching the fires that make no practical sense.

For this reason, Islam does not, like Catholicism and Buddhism, advocate celibacy as a way of life. According to tradition, a person fulfills half of his duties to Allah by marrying (by pairing) and the other half in worship and other rituals (e.g., prayer). In addition, one of the five "guarantees" in Islam is that of procreation. So, a Catholic tradition like celibacy would (logically) for the Prophet lead only to half of a fulfilling life, at best. Since the purpose of the sex act is not just pleasure and release from the itch of the sex drive, but also procreation, a way of life that does not involve sex and procreation, but shies away from it is not Allah's way.

Non-Sexuality

By the non-sexual form of sexual expression, we are referring to men who have been castrated and women whose genitals have been mutilated, so depriving both of normal sexual feelings and capabilities. However, since such women may still have children and thus can procreate, they are less restricted than the men.

While the Quran makes no mention of the practice of female genital mutilation, and is not practiced by the majority of Muslims, it is still practiced in some Muslim countries such as Sri Lanka, Malaysia, Egypt, Oman, Yemen and the United Arab Emirates.[47]

As for eunuchs, that is another matter. Harems were ruled by eunuchs throughout the slave dynasty of Egypt (1254-1811), in the Ottoman Empire (1300+), and in the Mongol Empire, which had a few thousand. While Muslims in general don't care for eunuchs, they still employed them for places such as the harem, and places in Indonesia still have them.

One of the principal reasons why Muslims do not generally embrace the practice of making eunuchs is that procreation is one of the guarantees of Islam. It follows that eunuchs, who cannot procreate miss out on one of these guarantees. In addition, since such men do not generally marry[48], they are unable to fulfill one half of their duties to Allah (namely, marriage). However, Muslim men are circumcised.

Summary

From the foregoing, we get an understanding of the Islamic conception of sexual expression, which is as follow:

- Maybe to non-sexuality (in females and men; eunuchs all right if non-Muslim men)
- No to Asexuality (abstaining from sex, unless there are good reasons)
- No to auto-amore (period)
- No to polymorph-amore (this is like monkeys and polytheists)
- Polygyny is the norm
- No to Polyandry
- Mono-amore is OK for men and women only (no man-to-man mono-amore is OK), but not normative

In this view, the theology and the laws allow polygyny (one man and many women) as the norm and allow mono-amore, if that is agreeable

---

[47] See http://www.geocities.com/WestHollywood/Park/6443/women/fem_circum. html.

[48] Eunuchs have been known to marry, however.

to both men and women. Otherwise, everything else is proscribed and forbidden.

Chapter 5

Hinduism

The theme of Hinduism is that only one form of sexual expression is acceptable. While Hinduism may have begun with a Pagan attitude of openness and pluralism, it has become today very patriarchal and restrictive in its views of legalized sexual expression.

What is Hinduism?

Hinduism is a world-view that is philosophically complex and hard to characterize. Currently, there are over a billion people (roughly one-fifth of humankind) who would identify themselves as Hindu, making this the fourth largest world-view in the world (after Paganism, Christianity, and Islam). It is also the worldview with the oldest tradition, going back at least five thousand years.

Excluding Paganism, which I have noted is pervasive and probably the most widely followed worldview, Hinduism is definitely the most pluralistic worldview on the planet. One of the cardinal maxims or sayings of those who follow this worldview is that "Truth is one, but the paths thereto are many." In the Bhagavad-Gita, this idea is stated so succinctly that it deserves no further exposition: "No matter which path a soul may take; if he follows it to the end, I, God, receive him."[49]

This being the case, there is no need to believe or convert to any single worldview (such as Islam or Christianity demand), but to follow the way to which one is most suited. Hinduism is a world-view that could be called a meta-worldview because it accepts or includes within its purview any worldview whatsoever, even those that are exclusionary and extremist.

Hinduism considers itself an unchanging tradition of tolerance and understanding and at the same time an evolutionary worldview that has changed over time.[50] Its most sacred, but by no means authoritative or revealed scriptures, the Vedas, describe the religious beliefs of the Aryans, which were definitely polytheistic. Yet today's Hindu accepts Brahman, the supreme being, that is one and indivisible. However, Brahman is revealed in an infinity of incarnations (each with an idol to personify it), hence this monotheism is married to polytheism. We thus find in Hinduism both the refined and subtle philosophies that one would expect of a synthesizing monotheism as well as a plethora of idols and other representations of the divine that one would expect to find in the most Pagan of worldviews.

We also find views and attitudes that derive from our oldest traditions and attitudes combined with beliefs that reflect more modern, though not necessarily more advanced, attitudes and beliefs.

---

[49] Alfred W. Martin, *Seven Great Bibles*, New York: Cooper Square, 1975, p. 58.

[50] Not everyone would agree with this. See http://www.hindu.org/ where the home page opens with a definition of a Hindu as follows. "Acceptance of the Vedas with reverence; recognition of the fact that the means or ways to salvation are diverse; and the realization of the truth that the number of gods to be worshiped is large, that indeed is the distinguishing feature of the Hindu religion." B.G. Tilak's definition of what makes one a basic Hindu, as quoted by India's Supreme Court. On July 2, 1995, the Court referred to it as an "adequate and satisfactory formula."

Polymorph-amore

In the Mahabharata, the great patriarch Bheeshma describes the evolution of monogamous marriage as having four stages, which he associates with the four Yugas in which the Rigveda has divided the development of Aryan man.

According to Bheeshma, during the Kritayuga stage there was marriage by Samakalpa (promiscuity). In the next age, there was marriage by Samasparsha (group marriage). In the next Yuga, the marriage form was called Maithuna (restricted marriage which included marriage within a Gotra or clan). Finally, in the Kaliyuga stage we have Dwanda (monogamous marriage).

Promiscuous Sexuality

In the earliest form of human sociality, sexual expression was what we today would call promiscuous.[51] At the stage when we humans were still hunter-gatherers, that is before the advent of the sedentary lifestyle that agriculture brought us, we were very much like the Bonobo monkeys that we resemble in 98 percent of our DNA, a collective society where all of us together were involved in hunting and gathering, socializing and procreating. Sexual expression took place between males and females, males and males, and females and females with very few restrictions, if any.

Early people obtained their food by gathering the fruits, seeds, and roots of plants or by hunting wild animals. People ranged over their territory, with base camps always close to fresh water and the hunters covering an area within a few days walk from camp. Their most valuable true possession

---

[51] The word promiscuity, like the word Pagan, is a judgmental term that is meant to indicate something that is un-praiseworthy. Unfortunately, there is no other comparable term that is neutral.

was knowledge of their territory. Survival depended on knowing where and at what times of the year the plants and animals upon which they depended could be harvested. Stone age hunting and gathering societies were thin on the ground with perhaps only 500 people in an area the size of Massachusetts. People lived in small groups of 20 to 50 individuals moving seasonally over the land from which they gathered their food.

A society based on hunting and gathering has to carry out its activities in a collective manner. Correspondingly, sexual life was also promiscuous. In the harsh environs, there was no accumulation of wealth for everything that was gathered or caught had to be consumed since there was no way of storing what was accumulated for any length of time. Property was not yet a concept associated with individuals, so whatever property existed was in the form of crude tools, made of stone and bone and this belonged to the tribe as a whole, as every member participated in the hunt, which was by nature a collective activity.

During this time, we were most likely worshippers of the Great Mother. Sex was expressed whenever and with whomever on a collective basis. Promiscuity being the norm, we could only know who our mothers were—never who the fathers were. Our fathers were all the men in the clan, so we belonged only to our mothers.

The Vedas (there are four of them, with the Rig Veda being the oldest) describe life and society in what appears to be a Pagan world of poly-morph-amore. The writings (poems, really) are dedicated to nature and her ways. This state of collective or indiscriminate sexuality is the oldest form of human and animal sexuality. While some people under certain conditions do revert to a promiscuous form of sexual behavior, Hindus in the modern day, while tolerant, would still regard this as an immature and unacceptable form of human sexual expression.[52]

---

[52] My guess is that this attitude is the result of the influence of the British. Certainly, Hindu men do not appear to be any less sexually interested than men elsewhere. Were it not for the "stiff upper lip" attitude of the British, my guess is that all of us would be less repressed than we are now.

Tantric Sexuality

One cannot really leave the topic of polymorph-amore in Hindu sexuality without dealing with the matter of Tantric sexuality. Tantric sex is a part of the Hindu mystical tradition, though there are also Buddhist and Taoist varieties. Non-religious or non-spiritual Tantra is just a cover for promiscuity and group sex. However, within the mystical tradition and when practiced as a spiritual discipline, Tantric sex may involve not only monogamous sex, but also the auto-amoric, poly-amoric, and polymorph-amoric varieties of sexuality.

Tantric worship services generally take the form of a sexual ritual featuring slow, non-orgasmic intercourse as a prelude to an experience of the divine. There are two schools of thought on how these worship services are to proceed: the right hand and the left hand paths. The right hand path is one in which the ritual is more or less seen as meditational or as a monogamous rite (performed by heterosexuals and homosexuals alike). The left hand path is one in which dozens or even hundreds of couples may engage in the ritual sex act at the same time, sometimes following the lead of a pair of teachers.

Since we initially defined sexual expression as being orgasmic in nature, and since Tantric sex is non-orgasmic, there is some question about whether or not this is really a form of sexual expression.

Poly-amore

Food, and the tools and methods used in obtaining food are closely linked with human evolution and development. Archaeologists suggest that the earliest hominids (human-like ancestors) were mainly vegetarians, but that hunting and the use of simple tools began about two million years ago. The long period from then until the development of more sophisticated tools is known as the Paleolithic or old stone. Modern Homo sapiens appeared on the scene about 40,000 years ago. Hominids and then humans obtained food by hunting wild animals and gathering the edible parts of plants. These methods continued until the gradual change from using wild species to domestication and agriculture about 10,000 years ago.

Once we moved from hunting and gathering and from the bounties that the earth itself provided us to a more sedentary lifestyle based on cultivation, we appear to have evolved a new form of sexuality and sexual expression that is best characterized as poly-amore.

The Vedas are filled with innumerable instances of Gods and seers making love to nymphs for sensual pleasures. In those ancient times, mono-amore was just an idea and natural love was given a free rein. There is one famous description of unintentional polyandry, and polygamy was a common phenomenon for a long time with kings and noblemen having more than one partner in their harems.

As far as same-sex relations are concerned, modern India is similar to the Christian West in its attitudes of disparagement and intolerance. However, a recently published book describes two thousand years or more of same-sex relations that have been pretty much openly accepted up until modern times. So, the issue is an open one.[53]

Polygyny

In the description of the caste system, which still bedevils India (though it was outlawed in the 1947 Constitution), we find a description of the accepted polygynous situation.

Four social levels distinguish Vedic culture. The Brahmins were the highly respected priestly class, though there really is no formal priesthood in Hinduism. There was also a regal/military class (the Kshatriyas), a class

---

[53] See Ruth Vanita and Saleem Kidwai, *Same-Sex Love in India: Readings from Indian History and Literature*, New York: St. Martin's Press, 2000.

of merchants and agriculturalist (the Vaishyas), and, lastly, the laborers or the untouchables (the Shudras). This class (varna) system finds its sanction in the Rig Veda, book 10, hymn 90:12, and it is also addressed, although less directly, in book 1, 113:6. However there are references to the various castes in other Vedic texts, namely the Yajur Veda and the Artharva Veda. It should be noted that in 1947 (CE), Article 17 of the Indian Constitution abolished the practice of untouchability in any form. However, this did little to remove the practice.

The members of the lowest caste, the menial workers, are allowed one wife. The caste made up of cultivators and merchants are allowed two, one from their own caste and one from the lowest caste. The warriors and nobility are allowed three wives, while the Brahmins, the highest class, are allowed four wives.

Indians who are Muslims legitimately practice polygyny, but the Hindu Marriage Act of 1955 completely reformed the law relating to Hindu marriage all over India and made monogamy compulsory among all classes of Hindus, no matter the caste, and this includes forbidding Hindus from converting to Islam just so they can have more than one wife. So, for the modern Hindu, poly-amore is not a legal option, though many Indian men frequent prostitutes.

Polyandry

In one story in the Mahabharata, five Pandava princes (brothers) are tricked into marrying one woman, thus providing us with a scriptural description of polyandry. Yet, this must be taken as a form of relationship that is still close to the promiscuity of hunter-gatherers, yet a step towards group marriages, which is beyond promiscuity. Yet, even at this stage the problem of paternity is unable to be resolved. And the way the story is presented, it is suggested that such a situation arises only by accident. So, we may surmise that polyandry is treated pretty much the same way it is treated by other "organized" religions, namely it is outlawed or severely restricted—and the reason for this is not that there is anything inherently wrong with the practice, but that it is the standard when the "Great Mother" reigned, and we can't have that, can we?

Mono-amore

The modern Hindu regards mono-amore within marriage as the only legitimate form of sexual expression, though this is probably more the result of the Hindu Marriage Act of 1955, which completely reformed the law relating to Hindu marriage all over India and made monogamy compulsory, than it is to any inherent propensity toward mono-amore.

Of course, Indians still follow many of the traditions that have arisen in the course of their long history, and some of these traditions indicate that while marriage may be made in heaven, it is a heaven heavily weighed on the side of men. For example, while a marriage unites a man and a woman and provides an institution for the development of both sexes, a woman is a non-entity apart from a man. And there are passages in the Bhagavad-Gita that clearly suggest that women are like children and have to be treated as such.[54]

Further, we have the institution of Suttee, admittedly outlawed but still practiced, where the wife jumps into the funeral pyre of her husband.[55] There is also the tradition of suspicion regarding widows—they cannot

---

[54] The Bhagavad Gita at 9:32 clearly suggests that men and women are equally capable of spiritual development, but Women are also thought to be untrustworthy and stupid, easily corrupted (1:40), and a hindrance to men on the path to liberation (16:11-12).

[55] One reason advanced for this is that it arose during war-time when there were many young women around and few men to give them a married life. However, Moslems solved this problem by allowing multiple wives (Mohammed married many widows late in his life).

remarry because virginity is prized in a wife, and if they do not marry then they are suspected of promiscuity (and thus of being whores).

Laying problems such as these to one side, marriage is regarded as the sole legitimate avenue of sexual expression for the woman and man, though women who "stray" are ostracized, while men who do the same are not. Men control the sexuality of women by channeling it into marriage and reproduction. All other forms of expression are regarded as promiscuous.

Auto-amore

Auto-amore, including masturbation, is something that Hindus don't talk about that much. In one of their traditions, we have a view of life as consisting of four stages: childhood and young adult, householder, householder with a mission, and ascetic. The ascetic is expected to focus on things other than sensual pleasures. The householder (second and third stages) is married and should not seek sensual pleasures outside his relations with his wife. And in the first stage, celibacy is expected. So, from their formal views of the stages of life, there is no place for auto-amore.

Of course, there is a Hindu myth that describes the phallic god, Shiva, being masturbated by Agni, the god of fire, who swallowed his semen. Agni then gave birth to Skanda, a god of male beauty. But this story is more a recognition of mutual masturbation than of auto-amore, so it is of dubious relevance to auto-amore. However, the Hindus, like later Buddhists, often denounced attachment to sexual pleasure as a cause of human suffering, so we may assume that they do not regard auto-amore as a legitimate form of sexual expression.

Asexuality

Hindus regard asexuality or celibacy as an ideal form of sexual expression. Celibacy is a lifestyle choice. Those who choose it do so because they want to focus their lives on things other than sensual pleasures. However, a celibate who voluntarily chooses to be such must learn to differentiate celibacy for the sake of seeking bliss from celibacy as an autonomous search for sensual pleasure (as in auto-amore).

Non-Sexuality

Genital mutilation of women is virtually unheard of in India, being practiced only by a small Muslim sect, but is unknown among Hindus.[56]

The case of male genital mutilation is, however, different. There exists about half a million Hijras, as male eunuchs are known. These people are generally eunuchs by choice. Being neither male nor female, they are in effect sexless, though they are called she or female in India. These secretive and shy people worship a mother goddess who demands infertility of her followers. This order admits neither men nor women to its ranks. Generally, they live together communally with a teacher, do not have families, and live celibate lives of service and celebration.[57]

Summary

From the foregoing, we get an understanding of the Hindu conception of sexual expression, which is as follow:

- Non-sexuality is OK among the Hijras.
- Asexuality is prized as a way to bliss and an escape from sensual pleasures.
- Auto-amore is probably practiced widely but is not a legitimate form of sexual expression.
- No to polymorph-amore (this was OK in pre-agricultural societies)

---

56 See http://www.amnesty.org/ailib/intcam/femgen/fgm1.htm#a3. Also of interest may be a map of male and female genital mutilation worldwide. See http://www.circum-stitions.com/aol/Maps.html.

57 See http://adaweb.walkerart.org/~vivian/jaffrey/~ for a review of a book by Zia Zaffrey called *The Invisibles*, which is about this cult.

- Polygyny is not acceptable.
- Polyandry is definitely not acceptable.
- Mono-amore is the norm (at least since 1955).

In this view, mono-amore and asexuality (celibacy) are prized, while the other forms of sexual expression are either forbidden or denigrated.

Chapter 6

Christianity

The theme of Christianity is that no form of sexual expression is good. If you must, choose mono-amore. Christianity is notably a dualistic worldview that has a sharp aversion to sensuality and to anything associated with the body. Of the six worldviews we have looked at here, Christianity is the next most restrictive in its view of human sexuality. Of all things sensual, sex is the most evil.

What is Christianity?

Christianity is a bizarre salvation cult that developed out of Judaism and a variety of Pagan cults that existed in Roman-controlled Judea two thousand years ago. Eventually, with the aid of various authorities it came to be the dominant worldview in the European world and from it in the Americas.

The Christian worldview combines the views of messianic Judaism with distinctively Pagan views and rituals, including ones with cannibalistic overtones (eating the flesh of the Savior at regular communion services) as well as vampire images (drinking the blood of the Savior in these same communion rituals). We also find hermaphroditic leaders (men dressed in skirts, as among the Catholic priests). In addition, most of its rituals and conventions, like Easter and Christmas holy days are taken over directly from Pagan sources.[58]

This worldview has at its apex a gendered god of the male sex who is distinctly identified as a father. This identification has a symbolic sense as God the Father, ruler of heaven and earth. But it also has a literal sense inasmuch as the father as an adulterous act conceived the child who was named Christ the Savior with the then childless Mary, wife of Joseph. Along with this illegitimate father-son relationship, we have another man called John the Baptist who presumably announced the coming or presence of the savior, and Saint Paul, a zealot and extremist. Moreover, all of the twelve disciples were men, though Jesus was supposedly on friendly terms with a number of harlots. In addition, the primary symbol of this worldview is the T-shaped cross that in Pagan systems is the symbol of the male member. The belief system is thus singularly a patriarchal system created by men, for men.

Further evidence of the primacy of men in this worldview is found in the place accorded women. In a variety of places in the Bible are to be found references to the way women are perceived and how they are to comport themselves. In Genesis, the fault for the fall into sin by eating the forbidden fruit is ascribed solely to the woman (Eve) leaving Adam blameless. From this beginning, we find that women are to cover their heads in worship, are to be silent, should never teach, and in most things are to subjugate themselves to men. For example, the noted misogynist, St. Paul, has this to say in Timothy 2:11-14 "Let the woman learn in silence with all subjection. But I suffer not a woman to teach, nor to usurp authority over the man, but to be in silence. For Adam was first formed, then Eve. And Adam was not deceived, but the woman being deceived was in the

---

[58] See Timothy Freke and Peter Gandy, *The Jesus Mysteries: Was the Original Jesus a Pagan God*, New York: Harper Collins, 1999

transgression." Elsewhere in Corinthians 14:34 "Let your women keep silence in the churches: for it is not permitted unto them to speak; but they are commanded to be under obedience as also saith the law. And if they will learn any thing, let them ask their husbands at home: for it is a shame for women to speak in the church."

The Judaic and Pagan origins of the Christian cult might give the impression that the cult preserved the openness to sexuality that is found in Paganism as well as the realism of Judaic views. That, however, is not the case. The idea developed within this worldview that anything to do with conception or copulation or sexuality or genital organs was evil or ugly. St. Augustine, probably the church's most influential theologian, wrote a little book on "Marriage" that includes passages portraying the Church's attitude towards sexuality. Even normal sexual intercourse within marriage can be for St. Augustine a venial sin, so even married people are urged to abstain from all sexual relations except when procreation is the sole purpose of the sex act. For Augustine all sexual acts or pleasure outside of marriage were mortal sins—acts sufficient to separate people forever from God and so consign them to hell.[59]

Polymorph-amore

In as few as words as possible, the view is "forget it." Nada. Zilch. No.

Polymorph-amore, many forms of loving, is just simply not acceptable within the Christian religion, ancient or modern. Many of the Christian missionaries who have gone out to "preach the gospel" in the last few hundred years have always chosen the Pagan societies (in Africa, Haiti, Latin America) as fertile ground for sowing their seeds. Pagan societies are, after

---

[59] All direct references to St. Augustine are taken from his little book on marriage that can be found at at http://www.newadvent.org/fathers/15071.htm.

all, often polytheistic, and if anyone has voiced disparagement of Paganism more than Islam, it is Christianity.[60]

Monotheists like the Jews or Muslims may be granted a dispensation of sorts, but Pagans and polytheists are simply wrong, sinners secure in the wrath of an angry god.

Pagans are an abomination for Christianity. Pagans are polytheists or atheists who do not accept the specific version of monotheism advanced by Christianity. As we have seen in our consideration of Pagans, followers of this worldview are apt to perceive all forms of sexual acts as natural and acceptable. For Christians, on the other hand, only sex that is intended for procreation and is performed within a monogamous marriage relationship is acceptable.

Poly-amore

The question of Poly-amore in Christianity is not as straightforward and non-controversial as one might suppose. First off, we must exclude homosexual men from consideration since men with men or one man with one man is considered an abomination. There is no explicit mention of lesbian relationships in the Bible. Nevertheless, Genesis 2:18, which has God saying, "It is not good that the man should be alone. I will make him a help meet for him," has been taken as a sign that men and women are acceptable companions for each other—but not men with men or women with women.

---

[60] Of course, the trinity (god in three persons) suggests that there is a polytheistic element in Christianity. Some have gone so far as to suggest that Christianity is a polytheistic religion. See, for example, http://members.tripod.com/ColoradoWeb/pantheon.htm or http://webpages.marshall.edu/~wiley6/polytheism.htm.

Polygyny

Polygyny is a very ancient practice found in many human societies. The Bible does not condemn polygyny per se. On the contrary, the Old Testament and Rabbinic writings frequently mention polygynous relationships enjoyed by men that God found favor with. King Solomon is said to have had 700 wives and 300 concubines (1 Kings 11:3). Also, King David is said to have had many wives and concubines (2 Samuel 5:13). The Old Testament does have some injunctions on how to distribute the property of a man among his sons from different wives (Deut. 22:7), however the only restriction on polygyny is a ban on taking a wife's sister as a rival wife (Lev. 18:18). The Talmud (like the Quran) allows a maximum of four wives. European Jews continued to practice polygyny up until the sixteenth century. Oriental Jews regularly practiced polygyny until they arrived in Israel where it is forbidden under civil law. However, under religious law, which overrides civil law in such cases, it is permissible.

The Christian view is found in the New Testament. In that part of the Bible, there is no mention of polygamy or polygyny. Moreover, Jesus does not speak against polygyny, even though the Jews of his society practiced it. The Church of Rome followed the views of the most influential theologian of Christianity (St. Augustine), Catholic or Protestant, who claims that in keeping with Roman custom, it is not acceptable to take more than one wife. However, the Church's ban on polygyny appears to be a cultural tradition and not an authentic Christian injunction.

Polyandry

Polyandry is another matter. It is supposedly a divine law that a woman is not allowed to have two husbands at the same time. In other words, she must wait until her first husband is dead before marrying a second. Nor is there a single example in the Scriptures of an Israelite woman who had two husbands at the same time.

In the New Testament, Romans 7:13, St. Paul says: "Know ye not, brethren, (for I speak to them that know the law) how that the law hath dominion over a man as long as he liveth? For the woman who hath a husband is bound by the law to her husband so long as he liveth; but if the husband be dead, she is loosed from the law of her husband. So then if, while her husband liveth, she be married to another man, she shall be called an adulteress: but if her husband be dead, she is free from that law; so that she is no adulteress, though she be married to another man."

A woman with more than one husband is an adulteress, but a man with more than one wife is all right under ecclesiastical law. In civil laws, in the West, however, one mate alone is allowed for either sex.

Mono-amore

Mono-amore we define as legitimate sexual relations between two people, regardless of sex. Within the Christian tradition however, we must immediately exclude relations between men. Leviticus 18:22 calls sexual relations between two men an abomination. Comparable statements aren't found about women, so we may presume that the Bible has nothing to say about lesbians as such. However, as already noted, it is taken as given that divine law intended men and women to be together and to have but one mate, so we may exclude lesbians also.

The Christian attitude about sex goes back hundreds of years to one great theologian, St. Augustine, who had a strong influence on the Church in his day and is widely regarded as the most influential theologian of the Christian church.

St. Augustine believed that Adam and Eve's problem in the Garden of Eden was sexual. He believed that the account of Adam and Eve's sin against God in Genesis 3 uses symbolic language and that the forbidden fruit actually represented sex. He thought Eve conceived and bore children in pain (Genesis 3:16) because sex is sinful, and any kind of sexual activity brings pain—if not immediately, then in the long run.[61]

According to St. Augustine, human beings should ask God's forgiveness for even thinking about sex and should abstain whenever possible. In fact, Augustine said that men and women who want to be righteous in God's sight should live in celibacy; that is without sexual contact. Marriage is the second best arrangement. The best arrangement is virginity ("…consecrated virginity is rightly preferred to marriage.").

Augustine's teachings give theological structure to feelings of guilt and shame in a biological drive. However, the enforcement of the doctrine of sexual guilt was difficult. The struggle was to impose celibacy on the clergy. It was only moderately successful until well into the Middle Ages.

Christians in his day as well as in ours have a hard time accepting Augustine's ideas about sex. They weren't certain that God wanted them to live in celibacy, yet his intricate arguments were hard to reason against. The church struggled to keep its leaders obedient to this rule. In fact, sexual prohibition was one of the first doctrines that Martin Luther and the other Reformers broke away from. Martin Luther, the proponent of Protestantism, left the monastery so he could marry a nun—yet he, too, regarded women simply as a vessel for procreation.

Auto-amore

There are no references to masturbation (auto-amore, self-pleasure) in the New Testament, though there are a few in the Old Testament. However, the church has historically viewed sexuality as having been designed only for procreation. As St. Augustine said, "The union, then, of

---

[61] St Augustine's view of sex and marriage can be found in *St. Augustine on Marriage and Sexuality* by Augustine, Elizabeth C. Clark (Editor), Catholic Univ of America Press; ISBN: 081320867, January 1977 or online at http://www.newadvent.org/fathers/15071.htm.

male and female for the purpose of procreation is the natural good of marriage. But he makes a bad use of this good who uses it bestially, so that his intention is on the gratification of lust, instead of the desire of offspring." Thus, sexual acts that cannot lead to conception are condemned as against natural law.

The same can be said about masturbation, self-pleasure. It does not lead to procreation, so it is against nature. In 1 Corinthians 7:4, St. Paul says "The wife hath not power of her own body, but the husband: and likewise also the husband hath not power of his own body, but the wife." In other words, the wife's body belongs not only to her, but also to her husband, and similarly the husband's body belongs not just to him, but also to his wife. Thus, all forms of sexual experience out of marriage is sinful, just as all forms of self-oriented sexual activity in and out of marriage are sinful and lustful rather than holy, loving and pleasing to God. Thus, fornication, masturbation, homosexuality, pornography and so on are sinful and a violation of the seventh commandment (which condemns adultery).

The overarching principle is that sex is for procreation and only within monogamous marriage. Since auto-amoric masturbation involves only one person, it is an abuse of this gift of God. Genesis 2:18 describes how God created sex to overcome man's aloneness. Thus, sexual intercourse was meant for two people. Masturbation thus goes against God's purpose for sexuality.

Asexuality

Though Genesis tells us that God does not think it is good for a man to be alone, which is why Eve was created, we do not find any condemnation of aloneness there. Many years later, St. Paul was to say, in 1 Corinthians 7:32-35 "He that is unmarried careth for the things that belong to the Lord, how he may please the Lord: But he that is married careth for the things that are of the world, how he may please his wife. There is difference also between a wife and a virgin. The unmarried woman careth for the things of the Lord, that she may be holy both in body and in spirit: but she that is married careth for the things of the world, how she may please her husband. And this I speak for your own profit; not that I may cast a snare upon you, but for that which is comely, and that ye may attend upon the Lord without distraction."

St. Augustine may have had a part in making celibacy a rule for priests and nuns. He says, "consecrated virginity is rightly preferred to marriage." This and many other reasons have been advanced for the cause of both male and female asexuality or celibacy and refraining from sexual relations. The Catholic church has made celibacy a requirement of the priesthood, though the frequency of sexual abuse and pedophilia among priests and the frequent pregnancies among nuns (and the many secret cemeteries for aborted or murdered babies) would make one want to question the realism behind such doctrines.

Non-Sexuality

Female genital mutilation is not practiced in those countries, mainly in the West, that practice state-sponsored religion, such as all of the Americas, Europe, Russia, Australia, the Philippines, and a few other places.

However, male genital mutilation is still practiced throughout North America in the form of circumcision, a Jewish form of genital mutilation that does not destroy all of the male's capacity for sexual pleasure.

Summary

From the foregoing, we get an understanding of the Christian conception of sexual expression, which is as follows:

- Yes to Celibacy
- No to Auto-amore
- No to Poly-amore
- Maybe to Polygyny

- No to Polyandry
- OK to Mono-amore
- Non-sexuality is abnormal and unnatural, though many men are circumcised at birth.

In this view then, only mono-amore (involving men and women) and celibacy are fully acceptable.

Chapter 7

Buddhism

The theme of Buddhism is that no form of any kind of desire is all right; however if you must, select mono-amore.

Like Christianity, Buddhism is a notably dualistic worldview that has a sharp aversion to sensuality and to anything associated with the body, which occupies the world of illusion and suffering. While Christianity is primarily adverse to the sensuality of sex, however, Buddhism is adverse to the entire world of sensuality.

What is Buddhism?

Buddhism is unique among the worldviews we are considering because it does not involve any theology. However, it is similar to Christianity in advocating a view of salvation. Since desire is the cause of all suffering, controlling one's desires is the way to attain salvation. Salvation is not dependent upon some external agent like a god or saving deity. The original Buddhism involved neither god nor devil. The emphasis was not on praying to some deity for salvation, but on controlling one's passions.

Salvation for Buddhism is attained with the experience of having conquered and subjugated one's desire (and hence one's suffering). This experience is called enlightenment. The Buddha began his teaching not with any dogmatic beliefs or mysteries, but with a valid, universal experience, which he presented to the world as a universal truth. The Buddha did not teach theories or beliefs. He always taught from practical experience based on his understanding of his enlightenment, and his realization of the truth. And his version of the truth is that the passions for pleasure, for existence, and for prosperity are the root causes of suffering.[62]

Buddhism began with the enlightenment 2500 years ago in the person of Gautama, the Buddha. When the Buddha introduced his teachings, his intention was to point out the futility of the worldly life, which is based on desire and seeking sensual pleasures, and to show the correct, practical path to salvation that he had discovered.

The Buddha described the practical basis for enlightenment (and hence salvation) on the basis of four virtues: (1) Saddha, which means that a person should have faith and confidence in moral, spiritual and intellectual values; (2) Sila, which means that one should abstain from destroying and harming life, from stealing and cheating, from adultery, from falsehood, and from intoxicating drinks; (3) Caga, that one should practice charity and generosity, without attachment and craving for wealth; and (4)Panna, which means that one should develop wisdom which leads to the complete destruction of suffering, to the realization of Nirvana.

We know that there were many enlightened ones, many Buddhas, before Gautama's birth and there have been many Buddhas after his death. The historic Buddha was born a Hindu and the evidence suggests that he wanted to reform Hinduism rather than reject it completely. Gautama died a Hindu, not a Buddhist, just as Jesus died a Jew, not a Christian.

What we call Buddhism today is an amalgamation of the true teachings of Gautama, combined with invented myths and large amounts of culture derived from whatever country Buddhism is practiced. Tibetan Buddhism,

---

[62] See Alfred W. Martin, *Seven Great Bibles*, New York: Cooper Square, 1975, p. 73.

for example, is as much Tibetanism as it is Buddhism. Buddha's words were handed down for several centuries through oral tradition before a committee was formed to commit the communal heritage, not memory, of Buddha's teaching to written form. No human being who actually met the Buddha wrote any of the famous Buddhist scriptures that present day followers take so literally and seriously.[63]

As far as sexual matters are concerned, Buddhism appears to be of two minds. Strictly speaking, since all sensuality and desire is "worldly" and a cause of suffering, which for the Buddha is something we need to escape from, sex is also something we should avoid if we are to escape the world and attain salvation from the constant circle or reincarnation. However, since we are also of this world and a part of it, our sexual expressions should be guided by the four virtues described earlier, and particularly by Sila, which enjoins us to avoid harming others and sexual misconduct.[64]

Polymorph-amore

The Buddha said that he had never seen any object in this world that attracts man's attention more than the figure of a woman. At the same time, the main attraction for the woman is the figure of a man. This means that by nature, woman and man give each other worldly pleasure. They cannot gain happiness of this kind from any other object. When we observe very carefully, we notice that among all the things that provide pleasure, there is no other object that can please all the five senses at the same time beside the male and female figures. This type of love is animal love or lust.

---

[63] This is also true of Christian teachings.

[64] While the following interpretation of Buddhism and sex is my own, I have profited from Bernard Faure, *The Red Thread: Buddhist Approaches to Sexuality*, Princeton University Press, 1998.

For animals, sex is just an instinctive drive necessary for procreation. But for a human being duties and responsibilities are important ingredients in maintaining unity, harmony and understanding in a relationship between human beings.

The second of the virtues (Sila) described above is directed against all forms of sexual misconduct, which include rape, adultery, promiscuity, and other sexual perversions. Actually, the Buddhist commentary emphasizes adultery more than anything else, but if we take into account the purpose and intention of the precept, it is clear that the precept is intended to cover all improper behavior involving sex. This virtue promotes, among other things, proper sexual behavior and a sense of social decency in a human civilization where self-restraint is a cherished moral value.

According to Buddhism, those who are involved in extra-marital sex with someone who is already married, or with someone who has been betrothed to someone else, and also with those who are under the protection of their parents or guardians are said to be guilty of sexual misconduct, because there is a rupture of social norms, where a third party is being made to suffer as a result of the selfishness of one or the other partner.

Such views would obviously preclude polymorph-amore from the domain of acceptable sexual expression. Animal love, lust or concupiscence may desire multiple sex partners, but not responsible humans.

Poly-amore

The Buddha did not lay down any laws regarding the questions of poly-amore in any of its forms. However, he did give advise on how to lead a respectable and responsible married life, and he also emphasized that one should respect the traditions and culture recognized by the majority in a particular country. So, if a religion practiced in a particular country allows multiple partners then presumably that is all right with Buddhism. Presumably, this also applies to men with men and women with women.

However, if we were to consider whether or not a Buddhist would even be allowed to live in a Muslim country that does allow polygamy, the answer would probably be no. Possibly in Tibet, where polyandry is practiced in some places, polygamy among Buddhists would be all right.

As in all other matters concerning sexual expression, Buddhists see the need for a sex life with a single spouse or with multiple spouses as a hindrance to the spiritual life. Those who get married, for example, do so not only to possibly procreate but also to satisfy urges that they cannot renounce.

Mono-amore

All living things come into being as a result of sex. Among human beings, the institution of marriage has come about so that society can guarantee the perpetuation of the human species and also to ensure that the young are cared for. This is based on the argument that children born through the pleasure of sex must be the responsibility of the partners involved, at least until they have grown up. And marriage ensures that this responsibility is upheld and carried out.

When one ceases to crave for sensual pleasure and does not seek to find physical comfort in the company of others, the need for marriage does not arise. Suffering and worldly enjoyment are both the outcome of craving, attachment and emotion. If we try to control and suppress our emotions by adopting unrealistic behaviors, we create disturbances in our mind and in our physical body. Therefore, we must know how to handle and control our human passion. Without abusing or misusing this passion, we can tame our desires through proper understanding. However, if we cannot tame our desires, then marriage may be in order.

From the Buddhist point of view, marriage is neither holy nor unholy. Buddhism does not regard marriage as a religious duty nor as a sacrament that is ordained in heaven. Marriage is basically a personal and social obligation and is not compulsory. Man and woman must have the freedom either to get married or to remain single.

Marriage, for Buddhists, is a partnership of two individuals and this partnership is enriched and enhanced when it allows the personalities involved to grow. In the Buddhist perspective, marriage means understanding and respecting each other's beliefs and privacy.

There must be no thought of either man or woman being superior—each is complementary to the other. Marriage is a partnership of equality, gentleness, generosity, calm and dedication. Knowing the psychology of the man who tends to consider himself superior, the Buddha uplifted the status of a woman by a simple suggestion that a husband should honor and respect his wife. A husband should be faithful to his wife, which means that a husband should fulfill and maintain his marital obligations to his wife thus sustaining the confidence in the marital relationship.[65]

Auto-amore

People are advised in the Buddha's teaching to avoid sexual misconduct. That means that if one wants to experience sex, one must do so without creating any violence or by using any kind of force, threat or causing fear. A decent sex life which respects the other partner (including oneself) is not against this religion because it accepts the fact that it is a necessity for those who are not yet ready to renounce the worldly life.

As a result, while all attachment is a cause of suffering and should be avoided, auto-amore is just another form of attachment to worldly things. But if one cannot control oneself, then auto-amore is as good (or as bad) as any other form of sexual expression.

---

[65] See http://www.enabling.org/ia/vipassana/Archive/D/DeSilva/WomenInBuddhism/ womenInBuddhismSwarnaDeSilva.html and http://departments.colgate.edu/greatreligions/ pages/buddhanet/theravada/women.txt for a discussion of the place of women in the Buddhist worldview.

Asexuality

Celibacy is refraining from the pleasure of sexual activity. Buddhism is not against sex itself, which is a natural, sensual pleasure and very much a part of the worldly life. However, the Buddha did support celibacy, for the same reasons that Christianity does. Being celibate for spiritual development was not a new religious precept at the time of the Buddha. All the other existing religions in India at that time also had introduced this practice. Even today, some other religions, like the Hindus and Catholics observe this as a vow.

Buddhists who have renounced the worldly life voluntarily observe this precept because they are fully aware of the commitments and disturbances that come along if one commits oneself to the life of a family person. The married life can affect or curtail spiritual development when craving for sex and attachment occupies the mind and temptation eclipses the peace and purity of the mind.

The Buddha recommended celibacy because sex and marriage are not conducive to ultimate peace and purity of the mind, and renunciation is necessary if one wishes to gain spiritual development and perfection at the highest level. But this renunciation should come naturally, and must never be forced. Renunciation should come through a complete understanding of the illusory nature of the self, of the unsatisfactory nature of all sense pleasure.

Non-Sexuality

Genital mutilation for either men or women is not part of the Buddhist religion.

Summary

From the foregoing, we get an understanding of the Buddhist conception of sexual expression, which is as follows:

- Yes to Celibacy
- Maybe to Auto-amore
- Maybe to Poly-amore
- Maybe to Polygyny,
- Maybe to Polyandry
- OK to Monogamy
- Non-sexuality is not practiced.

In this view then, only celibacy is fully acceptable, with marriage as a second best situation.

Chapter 8

Comparisons and Contrasts

Now that we have taken a look at six of the world's principal worldviews, we need to compare and contrast these views so as to see what may be gained from them to support a reasonable and sane sexual ethos that is suitable globally.

Negations of Sexuality

Though it is entirely unlikely that there ever was a time when Polymorph-amore reigned supreme and humans enjoyed unbridled sexual license, we can postulate such a time as a foil against which to compare the views presented by the worldviews we have considered.

The first and most obvious observation we can make is that excepting Paganism, which is a cultural representation of Polymorph-amore, all the other worldviews can be summarized as being negations of sexuality in some form or another. Where Paganism appears to be open, pluralistic, accepting and non-judgmental, all the other worldviews frown upon one or another aspect of the Pagan views of sexual expression. All of them are negations of the full spectrum of logical possibilities for that expression.

Where the worldviews differ is not over their attitude of negativity of the full spectrum of human sexual expression, but over which part of that spectrum they accept and which ones they deny. It appears that there is a universal experience expressed in the injunction to Adam and Eve in the biblical myth of the Garden of Eden where they were forbidden to eat of the fruit of the knowledge of good and evil. A divine "No!" seems to reside at the very heart of culture and the worldviews that underlie them.

Now, there are numerous studies presenting one or another theory about why various taboos, among them sexual taboos, arose in the course of human evolution. I have no wish to examine any of these, though they provide insight into the various causes and strategies that human beings used to get where they are today. However, I am not concerned with the theories of the possible strategies for the avoidance of sexual expression so much as with the fact that they exist in various worldviews.

So, let us consider what these different worldviews seek to avoid or accept. Where do they say yes and where do they say no, regardless of the causes or reasons or possible strategies involved.

Polymorph-amore

Anthropologists speculate that human beings have been around for about two million years, maybe more. From the start and continuing for all but the last ten thousand years or so, we were hunter-gatherers whose worldview, if we had one, was Pagan, and whose social structure was egalitarian and communal. This means, in effect, that for 99 percent of our existence, we were Pagans. Matriarchy was the rule of the day. Sex was natural and free. We lived and loved the way the rest of nature lives.

Of course, unbridled sexual license where men with men, women with women, and men and women with each other enjoy sexual expression is probably only a myth, a dream, but Paganism comes the closest to accepting it. Of course, in such a society, matriarchy would be the dominant form of authority since paternity cannot be determined where women have a right to engage in sexual acts with an unlimited number of different men.

Then at some point only a few thousand years ago, everything changed. Instead of nomads, we became sedentary. Instead of communal ownership, we started to enclose some portion of land and cultivate it and protect it from others. Instead of all women in a tribe belonging to all men, we started to affirm proprietary rights. And instead of unbridled sexual license, we started to limit and circumscribe our forms of sexual expression.

Polyandry

Polyandry is a key feature of the Pagan worldview. However, it is rejected by all the other worldviews except possibly by Taoism. However, it must be noted that the cultures of all the other worldviews support the civilly illegitimate practice of female prostitution, which is polyandry by any other name. And the practice of one woman having several different lovers is an ingrained part of the culture of most worldviews, and is certainly part of Western culture.

Polygyny

Polygyny is the practice of men having multiple female partners. This practice is common throughout the world, though only Islam supports it as a legitimate form of marriage. All the other worldviews frown on this, though there is nothing in Christianity, Taoism or Buddhism that specifically prohibit this practice.

Mono-amore

Mono-amore is institutionalized in all non-Pagan worldviews. Even Islam, which allows multiple wives, shows a preference for mono-amore. In 1955, India prohibited Hindus from having more than one wife. Throughout the Western world, one wife is the norm.

Auto-amore

Auto-amore, and specifically masturbation, is regarded ambiguously by the great worldviews. Buddhism, Christianity, Hinduism, and Islam are opposed to it. Taoism supports female masturbation, but thinks it should be restricted for men. Paganism sees it as one of the acceptable modes of sexual expression.

Asexuality

Celibacy, which is the avoidance of occasions for and the occurrence of sexual release made as a matter of choice, is treated differently in the worldviews. Islam and Taoism, for different reasons, say no, Paganism says maybe, and all the rest—Hinduism, Buddhism and Christianity are in favor of this mode of sexual expression. We presume that Paganism would say maybe because its pluralism and tolerance suggest that, though in all likelihood, it was accepted because of illness, lack of interest for various reasons, or some physiological dysfunction. Taoism objects to celibacy because it holds that sex with another (or even with oneself) has a positive benefit for health, while Islam avoids celibacy because sexual relations with women that lead to procreation is a guarantee, a virtue, in that religion—and no celibate can be a virtuous Muslim.

Non-sexuality

While Hindu India accepts the neither male nor female eunuchs, no other worldview supports the mutilation of male genitals to the point of emasculation, though the Christian West and Islam do support circumcision.

On the other hand, though not strictly supported by the worldview, some Islamic countries do practice female genital mutilation of a most heinous kind, as do many African countries.

Diversity of Forms of Sexual Expression

One question that we might raise is about the bases for these diverse views of human sexual expression. If we look at the various forms of social interaction that exist among our closest living relatives—the great apes of Africa, we find a similar diversity of sexual expression.[66]

Diversity Among Primates

As we know from studies of the primates—among which we humans are one—our genetic makeup is around 97 to 98 percent similar to them.[67] Consider the diversity in modes of sexual expression found among them.

---

[66] See http://www.geocities.com/willc7/bonobos.html where Frans B. M. de Waal, Ph.D., provides the following description of primate differences.

[67] See http://www.nih.gov/news/NIH-Record/04_18_2000/story02.htm where the author, Rich McManus, says that "There is a ubiquitous sugar molecule on the cells of humans that differs only by the lack of a single oxygen atom from a cousin sugar commonly found on cell surfaces of our nearest genomic ancestors, the great apes. Thus far, it is the sole genetic difference—species-wide—distinguishing man from chimp, orangutan, gorilla and bonobo."

Bonobo

Bonobo communities are peace loving and generally egalitarian. The strongest social bonds are those among females, although females also bond with males. The status of a male depends on the position of his mother, to whom he remains closely bonded for her entire life. Bonobos engage in sex in virtually every partner combination (although such contact among close family members may be suppressed). And sexual interactions occur more often among bonobos than among other primates.[68]

Chimpanzee

In chimpanzee groups the strongest bonds are established between the males in order to hunt and to protect their shared territory. The females live in overlapping home ranges within this territory but are not strongly bonded to other females or to any one male. Sexual interactions occur between females, between males, and between males and females.

Gibbon

Gibbons establish monogamous, egalitarian relations, and one couple will maintain a territory to the exclusion of other pairs.

Gorilla

The social organization of gorillas provides a clear example of polygyny. Usually a single male maintains a range for his family unit, which contains several females. The strongest bonds are those between the male and his females.

---

[68] See De Waal, F. and Lanting, F. *Bonobo: The Forgotten Ape.* Berkeley: University of California Press, 1997. Humans share 99.5 percent of their DNA with bonobos.

Orangutan

Orangutans live solitary lives with little bonding in evidence. Male orangutans are intolerant of one another. In his prime, a single male establishes a large territory, within which live several females. Each female has her own, separate home range. This is a form of polygyny.

Comparison to Human Worldviews

If we compare the human worldviews we have considered to the above list of primate sexual arrangements, we find that the differences among our primate relatives are as pronounced as are the differences among these worldviews. In addition, appeals to what is "natural" as made by the Church of Rome and other groups allied with Christian and related worldviews appear to be entirely specious. Mono-amore is as "natural" as polygamy or Pagan sexuality.

Pagans and Bonobos

The bonobo primate clearly resembles the Pagan worldview of sexuality. They are female centered (Goddess is primary), they are egalitarian, and sex is engaged in between females, between males, and between males and females.

Gibbons and Mono-amore

Gibbons with their tendency to mono-amore most loosely resemble Christian, Buddhist, and Hindu attitudes towards mono-amore. Regardless of the theologian's diatribes against being like the animals, the Christian or Buddhist or Hindu views that mono-amore is human, while anything else is sub-human, is just plain nonsense.

Chimpanzees and Poly-amore

Chimpanzee sexual expression appears to be less "Pagan" than the bonobos, but not as "Christian" as the gibbons. There appears to be a tendency to both polygyny and polyandry among the chimpanzees, thus putting them on the side of the Taoists.

Gorillas, Orangutan and Islam

Though the Prophet goes to great lengths in the Quran to castigate the ways of the monkeys and to prohibit Muslims from behaving like them, it would appear that the monkeys he had in mind were the bonobos rather than either gorillas or orangutans. I say that because the sexual arrangements of gorillas and orangutans resemble the sexual arrangements of Muslims. Muslims, orangutans and gorillas are all supporters of polygyny (one man with many women). The Prophet's diatribes against monkeys notwithstanding, Muslim sexual behavior resembles that of (some) monkeys.

What is the Basis for this Diversity?

That's a huge question, which I obviously cannot answer in principle, much less answer in this book. We all know that there are probably hundreds of thousands of reasons and causes for our human variability—genes, population, food availability, water, minerals, vitamins, and so on are all involved. However, given the fact that our primate cousins have evolved forms of sexual expression as diverse as our own, we have to wonder where our own diversity of worldviews on sex arose. Certainly, the gorillas and orangutans did not have a prophet telling them they could have multiple wives the way Islam does; nor did the gibbon have its resident theologian consigning them to hell and damnation if they were not monogamous the way Christians have said we should be.

So, regardless of the concept of divinity (or lack thereof) and regardless of the moralists and other busybodies in the world, human sexual diversity is probably no more the result of prophets and theologians than are the forms of sexual expression among the primates.

This fact at least suggests that we humans behave a certain way and find rationalizations after the fact. The rationalizations then serve to attract others to whatever the cause is that we're advancing. This observation is important for my purposes because I think we need a new global sexual ethos, but this ethos already exists among humans and a rationalization, such as I propose in the next chapter, will merely be stating the obvious.

Chapter 9

Towards a Global Sexual Ethos

While it may eventually be necessary for the human family to discover or develop a new worldview that can embrace the principles needed for a satisfactory global sexual ethos, my sense is that we have more than enough worldviews, more than enough religions, more than enough ideologies and partisan, tribalistic perspectives. What we need is not another worldview so much as a return to the worldview that governed our existence prior to the development of agriculture, namely Paganism.

Towards that end, I want, first, to describe what I believe are the strengths and weaknesses of the views of the worldviews we've considered here, then secondly, to describe problems that we face that need resolution. After that, I will describe the principles and policies for a global sexual ethos for the twenty-first century.

Strengths and Weaknesses in the Worldviews

In this section, I want to extract from the worldviews we have considered the principles or practices that can be carried over into a global ethos of sexuality.

Buddhism

What Buddhism considers to be its greatest strength and the key principle of its message to the world is in fact its greatest weakness, namely its distaste for and rejection of the cardinal feature of all life, which is conatus or desire. The entire objective of this worldview is not a "worldly objective" at all, but an attempt to have us convince ourselves of "the inherent nonexistence of phenomena" with the "goal of freeing ourselves from their suffering."[69]

Instead of facing up to the existence and fact of sexual desire, the Buddha bids us to hasten as far from it (and all other forms of sensuality) as we can get. If we are unable to do so, we may marry, but we should avoid all sexual misconduct including adultery, misuse of women, masturbation, homosexuality and other acts which create disturbance in the mind and in society.

Buddhism actually has nothing to give us towards a resolution of the problems attendant upon sexual desire. Its one commendable principle is that men and women are equal and should be treated with respect. This principle follows from the fact that for the Buddha the body (male or female) is of no ultimate consequence or importance. It does not matter for the Buddha what "body" wishes to renounce the world. This is a principle we can use in a global sexual ethos, but note that this is a principle that based on an unworldly sensibility.

Christianity

The views of Christianity concerning sexual desire are very close to those of Buddhism. For the proper service of God, we should renounce

---

[69] Dalai Lama of Tibet, *Essential Teachings*, Berkeley: North Atlantic Books, 1995, p. 79.

sexual expression altogether. However, since universal adoption of this principle would result in the extinction of the human species (which some people would regard as not all that bad), well then, marry (one person only)—or burn, as St. Paul said.

Unlike Buddhism that sees **all** desire as illusory, Christianity sees one overriding desire not as illusory but as evil and to be avoided. Like Buddhism, it would prefer celibacy or "consecrated virginity" as the highest calling, but will settle for marriage to one person, sex used for procreation, and the renunciation of all other forms of sexual expression.

Also unlike Buddhism, we find that this worldview subordinates women to men (it is, after all, a patriarchal system), so we cannot take from it the same principle of the equality of the sexes that Buddhism provides. In fact, I'm not sure that there is anything that Christianity can provide to a global sexual ethos.

Hinduism

Perhaps the greatest strength of Hinduism is its principle of the plurality of ways and its acceptance of a multiplicity of religious practices and worldviews.

It is unfortunate that it did not extend this principle to the forms of "marriage" and of sexual expression, but instead adopted the Roman-Grecian-European concept of a single spouse and monogamy.

It is also unfortunate that Hinduism did not extend equal rights to women and still, traditionally, regards women as derivatives of men. The practices of widow burning, for example, could have been more humanely resolved by allowing polygamy, or by accepting lesbian relationships.

Hinduism could do well to recall its polytheistic and Pagan roots and to re-think the narrowness it has come in its old age to accept.

Islam

One of the great strengths of Islam, in contradistinction to the triune polytheism of Christianity and its deification of a simple man, is that it recalled the people to a concept of a wholly unary godhead. Unlike the adulterous god of Christianity, Allah is wholly transcendent and has no consorts, no sons or family, and consequently is un-gendered (neither male nor female, neither father nor mother). As a consequence, there is no reason for Allah to favor any one of his creations over another, though apparently Mohammed thought that he should favor men.

While Islam has a powerful concept of god, it also has weaknesses associated with this concept. It is from this god, Allah, that men and women were created for each other. Men and women are equal in that they are sovereigns of their proper domains—the man in the public arena and the woman in the home. However, while Islam does grant almost equal status to men and women, it also holds that men are "above" women, just as Allah is "above" them both. This makes Islam just another patriarchy. And its insistence that women belong only in the home is an unnecessary prejudice.

Islam also holds that men may marry non-Muslim women, but that women must marry Muslim men. This is another unnecessary restriction. Had the Prophet really been consistent in his concept of god, he would have made men and women equal to each other.

Another inadequacy in Islam is its prejudice concerning the necessity of marriage and conceiving marriage as necessarily only between men and women. The Muslim concept of responsibility within marriage is certainly commendable, but this concept of responsibility needs to be extended so that it can encompass men with men, women with women, and men and women in groups in addition to the normal monogamous or polygynous concept of marriage.

Paganism

Paganism's greatest strength is in its polytheism, its tendency to infuse all existents with spiritual, divine qualities and in its acceptance of all things natural.

Paganism's greatest strength is also its greatest weakness. Accepting all of nature as alive and infused with divinity is a wonderful idea that gives support to treating the earth, Mother Nature, with respect and care. On the other hand, the human mind is incapable of thinking of more than six or seven things at the same time or of keeping more than six or seven categories aligned at the same time, yet in Paganism we are faced with an almost limitless variety of categories and divinities. Somewhere between the monotheism of Islam or Christianity and the infinite variety of divinity, we need a limitation, some principle of organization, which is not performed by the Great Spirit.

In effect, this mean that Paganism tends to be local, tribal, and provincial. What is local is taken to be what is universal, and particularly what is traditional within a locality. Locality and provinciality tend towards prejudice and tradition. The result is that the traditional may be interpreted as natural when it is only traditional. It is traditional for some African, Muslim societies to practice heinous forms of female genital mutilation—but that doesn't make it natural or all right. On the contrary, it is contrary to nature, chauvinistic, cruel, and inhuman.

That said, if we could somehow combine Paganism with science, openness with rationality, perhaps we could find a basis for a sound sexual ethos. Instead of calling us back to some proto-monotheism, as Islam wants to do, perhaps what we need is to be called back to a proto-Paganism.

Taoism

Like Paganism, Taoism brings the principle of naturalness and healthfulness of sexual release to the table. That said, its metaphysical calculus of yin and yang forces, and its identification of men with yang and women with yin, is inadequate. We know from science that men and women share "male" and "female" characteristics, with men having a higher percentage of maleness (55 percent) and women having a higher percentage (55 percent) of femaleness. Thus, to identify men with the yang force and women with the yin force is wrong.

That said, the Taoist argument against male homosexuality holds no water. Two women together are just as likely to be two "active" forces together as are two men. Similarly, two men together could just as easily be two passive forces or one active and one passive force together.

Similarly, the practice of sperm retention (particularly as men get older) is nothing but a technique for avoiding things like premature ejaculation and other forms of male behavior that leave women unsatisfied from their sexual couplings with men. On the other hand, the acceptance of female same-sex liaisons is commendable.

Problems we need to Address

Before going on to consider the changes we need to make in our modes of sexual expression if we are to have a global sexual ethos, we need to acknowledge that a new ethos is a solution to problems that exist. My sense is that our worldviews were (are?) all attempts to resolve certain problems and thus can be seen as solutions to problems. They did not spring full-blown from the mind of Zeus, so to speak, but arose in response to perceived problems in an existing society. Certainly, this is true of Buddhism and Islam. It is probably true of Taoism and Christianity. It may be true of other worldviews as well.

Acknowledge Sexual Desire

Paganism, Taoism, and Islam accept the fact of sexual desire and seek ways to satisfy these fires. Buddhism, Christianity and to a lesser extent

Hinduism, have misgivings bordering on paranoia concerning sexual desires.

Any suitable global ethos of sexual expression thus needs to adopt the realism of Paganism, Taoism and Islam, but reject the views of Buddhists, Christians and Hindus on the matter.

Children without Parents

One of the pressing problems faced by any society is the existence of children without parents to nurture and care for them. Anyone who has been to or heard about the hordes of young children who roam the cities of Latin America, as in Brazil or Columbia, must surely realize that this is a major problem of our day. But not just south of the border, but right here in the US, hundreds of thousands of kids run away from home and join the vast underground of exploited workers in the cities, many of them subjecting themselves to sexually transmitted diseases at the hands of predatory adults.

One of the great strengths of Islam is the requirement that children not be orphaned and that women not have children without a family support system. Surely, we can see the ills brought about by a system of monogamy coupled with prostitution.

Epidemics of STIs

Sexually transmitted infections are epidemic worldwide. Black Africa is dying from AIDS. Asian countries are seeing epidemics of STIs. STIs are common throughout the world.

A root cause of the spread of STIs is the sexual drive. While some people may want to eliminate the drive, or blame people who become infected (for example, Jerry Falwell blames homosexuals for the infections their behavior leads them to acquire), a more suitable response would be to improve the prophylactics that people could use against the possibility of infection, and institute medical testing for all "promiscuous" sexual activity.

While finding ways of preventing the spread of AIDS and other STIs may sound reasonable, there is great opposition from the Roman Catholic worldview and others like it. For example, in southern Africa where it is thought that HIV infects at least twenty percent of the population, governments have tried in vain to get the Catholic church to accept the use of condoms as a way to fight infection. Yet, the church opposes this move because they think that the problem is a moral rather than a medical problem.[70] The Catholic church is guilty of genocide.

Bases for a new Sexual Ethos

Though Muslims and Christians, primarily but not exclusively, will no doubt raise a hue and cry, the fact is that neither of these two worldviews is sufficiently universal to be able to serve as the basis for a worldview that can find the allegiance of all the peoples in the world. The same holds true for the other worldviews—Hinduism, Buddhism, and Taoism. All of these worldviews have something to contribute to the stew, perhaps, but none of them alone is sufficient.

We desperately need a new sexual ethos for the world—but I don't necessarily think that we need a new worldview or religion or ideology. If we had remained in our own little tribal or ethnic worlds and there had been no cross-cultural fertilization such as we find in the developing "global" society, then perhaps the several worldviews we have considered could all continue to exist in their own ecologies. However, whether we like it or not, we are evolving a global society.

The problem, however, is that the current model of the global society is dominated by the West and has evolved institutions like the United

---

[70] See http://news.bbc.co.uk/hi/english/world/africa/newsid_1465000/1465326.stm.

Nations that do not represent the best interest of all people, but only of a few. The same can be said about the worldviews we have considered, all of which assert that they are "universal," yet fail to be so.

If we are to have a new sexual ethos such as outlined above, we need changes in our declared values and changes in civil laws throughout the world. The following sections will describe some of the changes we must have.

The View of the Family

Other than the fact that the UN's 1948 Universal Declaration of Human Rights, which advances a common standard of achievement for the world community, is ignored by the majority of nations, including the United States and other world powers, one thing is quite evident in it—it is a set of standards that are based on ideas that are common to the West, specifically the Christian West, and does not bear witness to either science or cultural (or worldview) diversity.

Consider Article 16, which says: (1) Men and women of full age, without any limitation due to race, nationality or religion, have the right to marry and to found a family. They are entitled to equal rights as to marriage, during marriage and at its dissolution. (2) Marriage shall be entered into only with the free and full consent of the intending spouses. (3) The family is the natural and fundamental group unit of society and is entitled to protection by society and the State.[71]

This article, like most of the other articles in the Declaration is riddled with unwarranted assumptions and hegemonic statements.

---

[71] See http://www.un.org/Overview/rights.html.

What is a Family?

First of all, Article 16 says that "men and women of full age" found a family. Since we know on a factual basis that women alone and men alone may found families, this statement begs the question. Similarly, two or more men together or two or more women together may found a family—and have done so. So, this is an unnecessary and unwarranted restriction on the concept of a family.

We also know that the structure of families differ considerably from this definition. We have cohabitation, where no marriage is involved; single-parent families; stepfamilies; and extended families. None of these involve a man and a woman in a marriage relationship.

Family as the Fundamental Unit of Society

A second major assumption that this article makes is that the family, as defined, is the fundamental unit in a society. Again, this is factually or scientifically false. There are many "units" in a society, none more or less fundamental than the others. There are individuals, there are associations, and there are institutions.

A New Concept of Family

Given the many different structures that families may take, a few of which are mentioned above, and given that neither marriage nor a pair of male and female may be involved, Article 16 of the UN's Declaration must be rejected.

We need a new concept of the family that can encompass the variety of associations of a more-or-less ongoing nature in which individuals of both sexes may engage. We need a concept of family that includes not just different-sex couples, but also same-sex couples as well as groups of such individuals. Without ignoring the many complications for civil law that are involved in a general concept of the family, we need to redefine the family to mean any social group linked by affection, shared daily lives including sex, and mutual responsibilities. Such a definition can encompass the variety of forms of sexual expression that we have identified in this book.

This concept of the family can serve to unite the different concepts of marriage that we have found among the worldviews. This revised concept can be used to characterize the mainly group "marriages" that may have been characteristic of Pagan societies. It also includes monogamy as well as polygamy. And it can accommodate even singularities and auto-amore arrangements. It also includes non-heterosexual people.

Article 16 of the Declaration of Human Rights thus needs to be amended to read: (1) Men, women, or men and women of full age, without any limitation due to race, nationality, religion, or sexual orientation have the right to marry and to found a family. They are entitled to equal rights as to marriage, during marriage and at its dissolution. (2) Marriage shall be entered into only with the free and full consent of the intending spouses. (3) A family so constituted, whether of man-to-man, woman-to-woman, man to woman, or a plurality of these, is entitled to protection by society and the State.

Need to Reject Monogamy

A second thing that needs to be revised if we are to have a global sexual ethos is the concept that dominates Hindu, Buddhist, Christian and other cultures, namely that monogamy is normative. We need to legalize polygamy (that is, both polygyny and polyandry). Women should be able to have more than one husband, and men more than one wife. Legalized polygamy, coupled with legalized prostitution, would give a world culture a more natural sexual environment. Consider some reasons in support of this claim.

Monogamy is Dishonest

Wherever monogamy is practiced or is the civil law, which is all over the Western world or wherever Western influences prevail, monogamy is the law, but polygamy is the practice. Western societies have made it illegal to have more than one wife with laws against bigamy. The practice, however, is of serial polygamy (marriage, divorce, marriage, divorce…), or legal polygamy (wife plus mistress).

This is pretended monogamy. In reality, what we have here is polygamy without responsibility. The wife or mistress and the children may be cast off when the man is weary of them. The male has no responsibility for the future of his mistresses, and no responsibility for his divorced wife (beyond some limited alimony in some cases), and many men in the West avoid responsibility for their children. Ex-wives, ex-mistresses, and children are a hundred times worst off than are the wives and children in a responsible polygamous home.

Monogamy and Population Disparities

For many reasons, women tend to outnumber men. In the United States, there are around ten million more women than men. In many countries, the ratio of men to women is 1 to 1.2 or 1.3. Wars are one cause that the number of women exceeds the number of men.

The imbalance in the number of women to men can be resolved by celibacy and abstinence, which never work, or by female infanticide, which is practiced for example in China, or through the current norms in monogamous societies—sexual license without responsibility, prostitution, vast epidemics of sexually transmitted infections (like AIDS), and irresponsible childbearing all placing unmanageable burdens on the society.

Monogamy as Unnatural

Another reason for rejecting monogamy in favor of polygamy is that monogamy is unnatural. Monogamy is not the way we animals have developed and behave.

In *The Myth of Monogamy: Fidelity and Infidelity in Animals and People* by husband and wife co-authors David P. Barash and Judith Eve Lipton, the authors suggest that cheating on one's spouse is the rule in nature—not the exception.[72] If anything is unnatural, it is the practice of monogamy. There is no evidence from biology or anthropology, that monogamy is somehow natural or normal for human beings.

On the other hand, regardless of the worldview that may dominate in a culture, there is no evidence that monogamy works most of the time. Even Islam, which allows men but not women to have up to four spouses, is no exception. Saudi kings or princes, for example, may have four wives at a time, but they usually end up having many more wives than that over a lifetime. And Saudi men, even those with multiple wives, are known to be frequenters of the whorehouses of Yemen and Dubai.

Monogamy as Unrealistic

A final reason for rejecting monogamy follows from the previous reason. Monogamy is unrealistic for it does not work. As the wit said, "Polygamy is having one wife too many. The same can be said for monogamy."

Monogamy is an exceptional condition and not a rule. Two people (two males, two females, or a male and a female) may be so attracted to each other that a monogamous relationship can be maintained for a while. However, to require that it be so is not realistic. Men and women generally prefer multiple sexual partners—variety is, after all, the spice of life.

Polygamy as Natural, Realistic and Humane

Polygamy should be legalized in the US and throughout the Western world, as well as globally. This legalization would accept monogamy but permit polygamy in both senses. This would be a natural, realistic and humane policy.

---

[72] Published by W. H. Freeman Company in 2001.

Polygamy is natural and realistic. A cross-cultural analysis by anthropologists of 853 societies showed that 83% of them are polygynous, even where it is legally prohibited. In addition, it found that there are an estimated 25,000 to 35,000 polygynous marriages in the US. One study of 437 financially successful American men found that some had two separate families, each unknown to the other.[73] Polyandry (one female with multiple males), on the other hand, is known to exist mainly in agricultural and pastoral societies, but is rarely found in hunting communities.[74] On the other hand, one female with multiple males is a common and frequent occurrence wherever prostitution is practiced (is there anywhere that it is not?) and also in Western societies where such relationships do not require legal sanction.

Granted, there are people who argue that polygamy **as currently practiced** throughout the world is inherently hurtful to women.[75] This cannot be denied. But in many ways, the reason that women are hurt is not because of polygamy so much as because their rights are not protected by their societies. Wife beating cannot be an argument against polygamy inasmuch as wife beating occurs in a monogamous relationship as well in those societies that condone such behavior.

Consequently, it must be asserted most strongly that when I advocate polygamy as a legalized norm of relationship worldwide, I do so only with the proviso that men and women must be equally able to engage in such relationships, free of coercion and other male-on-female violence.

Just as there are those people who oppose polygamy because they believe it is enslaving of women, so there are others who would claim that

---

[73] David Buss, *The Evolution of Desire*, New York: Basic Books, 1994, pp. 177-178.

[74] Donald Symons, *The Evolution of Human Sexuality*, Oxford University Press, 1979, p. 225.

[75] See http://www.polygamyinfo.com/world_news.htm, where the idea is presented that two billion women are enslaved by polygamy.

it is in fact liberating to be able to enter into polyandrous and polygynous relationships. One argument in support of polygyny is that it in fact protects the interests of women and children in society. Men, however, make the laws and they prefer to keep polygamy illegal because it absolves them of responsibility for their offspring—beyond possibly paying for an abortion. Legalized polygyny would require men to spend their incomes on their additional wives and their offspring. Monogamy currently allows them to enjoy extra-marital affairs without economic consequence.

Another argument in support of polygyny is that institutional polygamy prevents the spread of diseases like Herpes and AIDS. Such venereal diseases are spread in promiscuous societies where extra-marital affairs abound. Polygynous relationships may thus inhibit illicit extra-marital relationships and thus STIs.

Yet another argument in support of polygyny is that given the disparity between men and women in most societies (there being more women than men), polygyny allows women who would otherwise exist in single-parent households, as well as widows and spinsters to enjoy the benefits of family life. This argument would weigh against polyandry because it would only decrease the pool of available men.

De-legitimating Genital Mutilation

As we have seen, female genital mutilation is practiced in various parts of Africa and in some, but not all, Muslim societies. As a universal right, it should be declared and legalized by all civil societies everywhere that such practices are to terminate forthwith. Any individual who engages in such activity should be held accountable to and provide recompense to the woman so mutilated—and in the case of men who perform such barbarism, they should be castrated and endure life imprisonment.

Male genital mutilation is a less general practice. Some men in India are completely castrated and must be so castrated if they are to become members of the Hijras sect, which allows neither men nor women as members. If this is a genuine, rational, mature choice of the men involved, the practice should be allowed to continue.

In the United States, and in a few other Western societies as well as in Islamic countries, many men are still circumcised either at birth or shortly thereafter.[76] One of the principal reasons given historically for this practice was to separate one community from another. Those who were circumcised were regarded as pure, separate, regenerated. Those who were not circumcised were regarded as degenerate, anti-authoritarian, undisciplined, impure, unclean—and immersed in a lifelong habit of masturbation, the reason being that the part of the penis that is circumcised (cut off) is very sensitive sexually.[77]

This practice of circumcision should be outlawed. However, if men, for whatever reason, wish to be circumcised later in life, after reaching the age of majority, they should be allowed to do so.

Promotion of Auto-amore

It is said by the wag that if asked discretely and in private, "Ninety-nine percent of people will admit to masturbation—and the other one percent are liars." While only Masters and Johnson may have accurate statistics on this, we can say with assurance that one hundred percent will not talk about it.

It really is time that we acknowledged that Jocelyn Elders, who advocated teaching women how to masturbate as a way of lowering the "illegitimate"

---

76 See http://www.cirp.org/library/ethics/denniston/. In Canada, the standard rate is down to less than four percent. In the US, while 90 percent were circumcised in 1980, by 2000 the rate was down to around 60 percent. The entire practice should be stopped.

77 See http://nocirc.org/symposia/first/riner.html for a description of the history and rationale of this practice.

birth rate in the US, was right and should be proclaimed as a national hero. Were it not for our weak and hypocritical presidents, including the one who fired her for making this suggestion, a solution to a pressing national problem would have been found.

In addition, we have the problems caused by STIs, sexually transmitted infections, of which AIDS is a major problem. When faced with a problem like this that is causing the decimation of various societies, particularly South Africa, which has the largest percentage of AIDS sufferers in relation to its population in the world, we need solutions—not more moralistic claptrap. If we were to teach people that sex is natural and that sexual release is also natural—and that one way to achieve this release without the consequences of either pregnancy or STIs is through auto-amoric practices like masturbation, what is wrong with that?

But there's more. We have almost one-third of the US population that is single and perhaps not enjoying any relationship, many of these widows and widowers or retired people. Why should they, too, not enjoy a satisfactory life of sexual enjoyment? Teaching people to masturbate should be as common as teaching them how to exercise or how to dance.[78]

Dissemination of Contra-infectives

The majority of sex education in the United States consists of abstinence-only sex. The idea is that everyone should abstain from sex until marriage, then within marriage one will not have to worry about STIs, assuming, of course that both partners are "faithful" and do not stray into extra-marital liaisons. If one is Catholic, one should not use contraceptive devices, since sex is for procreation (I'd guess that most US Catholics

---

[78] See Sue Johanson, *Sex is Perfectly Natural, but not Naturally Perfect*, New York: Penguin, 1991, pp.95-123. See also http://www.mypleasure.com/education/sexed/masturbation.asp.

ignore this injunction); if one is protestant, one may use contraception. If one gets an STI, it is because one has not followed this prescription (abstinence, then fidelity within marriage).

Unfortunately, while the religious right may keep its head in the sands over abstinence, the fact is that people engage in sex acts and need to know what they entail. And sad to say, most human sex is not used for procreation, and married people are rarely faithful, so STIs are always a problem.

While there are numerous ways of preventing conception, these are not my concern here. Many ways of preventing conception, such as hormonal methods (the pill) and barrier methods (condoms, vaginal sponges, foams, and so on), do nothing to prevent the exchange of bodily fluids or skin-to-skin transmission of STIs. The UN's WHO, for instance, has found that condoms are effective in preventing HIV infections and gonorrhea, but do not prevent skin-to-skin STIs.[79]

I certainly think that we need full-blown sex education in this country on all forms of sexual expression and on all varieties of STIs—as well as information on how to help prevent these infections. Research also needs to be performed to discover additional or better ways of infection prevention. For example, while condoms may be effective, they are not always available, they are expensive (say for someone in a developing country), and above all they are often desensitizing. Interpersonal sex with a condom is like eating without a tongue—no feeling in one case and no taste in the other. Why then bother?

A vaccine against all STIs would, of course, be ideal. But until this is found, especially for the life-destroying forms like AIDS that cannot be fought with antibiotics, we need to find and make available to all people better barriers to the transmission of STIs. A technology that can develop

---

[79] See http://www.who.int/HIV_AIDS/Condoms/effectiveness_of_condoms_in_prev.htm.

a blanket that is less than a millimeter thick can surely develop a condom that is not desensitizing.

Absolute Equality of Women

In the days when matriarchy prevailed and when men were nothing more than the bearers of the of the seeds for the next generation, it is quite obvious that men were merely the playthings of the women—objects to be patronized and treated merely as sex objects. Let's grant that. Then, when men became predominant, they returned the favor and through their religions and worldviews, treated women as mere objects, playthings, merely wombs for bearing the next generation. OK. Turnabout, as they say, is fair play. But enough, already.

Let's grant that men are from Mars and women are from Venus. Let's grant all the perceived and researched differences between men and women. Is that any reason for creating a legal and ontological barrier between the two sexes? Is there any rational basis other than revenge for treating women the way they are treated in the cultures dominated by the worldviews we've considered?

Is there any rational basis for treating women as mere appendages to men the way Hinduism conceives of them? Is there any basis for making men the actors in the public sphere and limiting women to the private sphere the way Islam does? Is there any rational basis for claiming that women must "submit" to men the way Christianity does? If you can think of a good reason, let me know because I cannot.

In any rational and global ethos of human sexuality, men and women must be accepted as equals—no ifs, ands, or buts. If men want to stay home and take care of the household—let them. If women want to go out into the business world and make their mark—let them.

Legitimating Same-sex Relations

It's been found that roughly ten percent of the men and women in any reasonably sized group will be inclined towards same-sex relations. This applies to men with men and women with women.

Now, why on earth would one want to deny these natural inclinations an expression? We already have more than enough people in the world, and even if we didn't, what is the harm in letting people who are so inclined express themselves in that way? Surely it is obvious that women are more caring and emotional than men, so why would we want to deny two women the right to express to each other the feelings of love and affection? I mean men are no great shakes when it comes to feeling or affection. Very few men have a clue about what either of these two affectivities involve.

And the same goes for same-sex relationships between men. So what if two men wish to fellate each other? What if one wishes to ejaculate his semen into another's anus? What of it? What's the big deal? What if two women wish to pleasure each other? Again, what's the big deal?

Definitely, the possibility of an STI is a consideration, but it is a consideration also for other-sex couples. And the problem of procreation is silly beyond comprehension. The entire business of procreative sex is based on a lot of what-ifs and maybes. When male fish spread their sperm upon the waters, it is pure possibility that some female will become impregnated. Even sex between two other-sex humans does not automatically result in procreation. It's all a matter of luck or chance. Most of the sperm generated by men, even if it is inserted into women, goes to waste, so why should that stop same-sex relations?

Even if there were but two human males left on earth and a multiplicity of women, there would still be no basis for denying the men and the women the right to same-sex relations—so long as men-women relations took place occasionally to assure procreation.

Legitimating Prostitution

Sexually transmitted infections (STIs) are epidemic worldwide. One STI, the HIV virus that is alleged to cause AIDS is decimating the continent of Africa. HIV/AIDS is also epidemic in Asia, the West Indies (e.g., Haiti and Grenada), as well as the Americas and Europe. Other forms of STIs, such as syphilis, genital warts, and many other forms, are epidemic throughout the world.

One of the principal reasons for the spread of STIs is the practice of unprotected (unsafe) sex with prostitutes. The only form of safe sex is auto-amore. We have already argued that auto-sexual practices such as masturbation should be taught and encouraged worldwide. We have also argued that contraceptives of all kinds should be made available worldwide and people should be educated in their use.

However, given the urgency of the sexual itch, people since time immemorial (isn't that why we call it the world's oldest profession?) have been sex workers and have exchanged sex for favors, particularly money. Having sex with unprotected men or women who may be carriers of STIs is a sure way of spreading STIs. If protection isn't used, then the only way of minimizing the risks associated with prostitution is to legalize and regulate the industry—and to have sex workers checked regularly for STIs.

The United Nations, in August of 1998, called for the worldwide regulation of sex workers. Many nations have signed up, but as usual, the backward and recalcitrant United States has not (just as it has not signed up to the Kyoto Protocols on global warming).

The US is one of the few nations in the world that refuses to legalize and regulate sex workers. Instead, untold sums are spent rounding up men and women who sell their bodies to others for sex, only to release them back onto the streets in a few days or hours—and nothing is done to make sure that they are not infected with STIs. The US satisfies its moralistic ignorance but does nothing to minimize the risk of infection to its citizens.

There are other nations that are similar to the United States in this regard. Though Muslim states condemn prostitution, most of them still allow the practice to continue. Bahrain and Dubai are two notorious examples of Muslim states where prostitution is illegal but where it flourishes because Saudi and Kuwaiti men, primarily, wants some way of escaping from the puritanical restrictions in their own countries.[80] However, these states are not alone. The sex trade flourishes in Iran, Indonesia, and elsewhere in the Muslim world. The Ayatollah Khomeni, leader of the Islamic revolution in Iran, was a noted misogynist who hated women, yet he legalized the practice of temporary wives (mutia) whose status may last only a few minutes.[81]

It appears that the most puritanical of states—The US and the Muslim countries—are the ones most likely to punish the crime of prostitution, yet leave the "sinner" unprotected from the consequences. The US needs to become enlightened, like the countries in Europe, particularly the Netherlands, Australia, and Canada—and legalize prostitution.[82] Unfortunately, this will not happen in my lifetime or yours.

---

[80] See http://www.muslimedia.com/ARCHIVES/oaw98/dubai.htm.

[81] See http://www.sharif.org.uk/iran.htm. We may deride the Taliban of Afghanistan, yet they had a great deal to do with eliminating the sex trade in that country. In these years of constant war under the Northern Alliance, Afghan girls were kidnapped on their way to school and sold to wealthy landlords in neighboring Pakistan. Warlords, upon conquering a territory, albeit briefly, would frequent the homes of the populace in search of young girls to use as sex slaves, some far below the ages of puberty.

[82] See http://www.consumer.vic.gov.au/bla/blasite.nsf/pages/bla_prostitution for information on what Australia requires of its sex workers.

Is Religion an Evolutionary Mistake?

When I began the research for this book, it was with the assumption that some synthesis could be made of the various principles that support the six different worldviews to arrive at solutions to sexual problems that plague us. Now, at the end of the journey, I rather think that I made a false assumption. It is not possible to synthesize or reconcile the diversity of views represented by the different worldviews into a global worldview.

In fact, I'm beginning to wonder if all the worldviews we have considered, with the exception of the proto-worldview of Paganism, were not humungous mistakes.

Paganism is a free, open, egalitarian, worldview based on the communal sociality of a hunter-gathering civilization. Up until about 10,000 years ago, all of us organized in small groups foraged for wild foods. For 99 percent of the time of humans on earth, we have been hunter-gatherers; only one percent of the time (over the last 10,000 years) have we been sedentary agriculturalists. [83]

For 99 percent of our existence, we lived a life of freedom, relative leisure, sharing, and openness to the "gods". But for the last one percent of our existence, we have moved from a culture dependent on a multiplicity of fruits and animals to monoculture; from diversity to restriction; from wandering to staying put—and from Paganism to a variety of rather horrific religions and worldviews. We were once extremely mobile. Then we made a massive turn to the white picket fence and a fixed address that we could call our own, and defend from all others.

It appears that it is with agriculture that we invented social hierarchies. Instead of communal ownership of the means of production, we became

---

[83] Information about this transition can be found in Charles Keith Maisels, *The Emergence of Civilization : From Hunting and Gathering to Agriculture, Cities, and the State in the Near East,* London: Routledge and Kegan Paul, 1993.

selfish, thinking in terms of my plot of land and my produce as distinct from yours. And this carried over to "my" children as distinct from yours—and "my" woman or women as distinct from yours. Power, control, ownership, privacy—and restrictive worldviews—all appear to be the product of our sedentary, agricultural lifestyle. So, I wonder, too, if agriculture wasn't a mistake along with restrictive religions and worldviews.[84]

Certainly, the five worldviews other than Paganism that we have looked at cannot carry a candle to Paganism. If we could find a way to jettison the other five worldviews and return to a Pagan worldview, we would have found a way to resolve a majority of the sexuality-caused problems that face us as a species.

In fact, the more secular civilizations that we are developing in the West seem to combine Paganism with rationality, though our legal system and institutions (not to mention attitudes and prejudices) still are combined with religious dogmas. It may well be that science will help us to regain our good sense along with the open, pluralistic, anti-authoritarian Paganism that was our common pre-history—and is our only hope for a common future.

---

[83] See http://fargo.itp.tsoa.nyu.edu/~jamie/philo/agriculture.html where the writer says: "I believe that humanity began its downfall—oppression of itself, other animals and the environment—when it began to subsist on large-scale agriculture."

About the Author

Derek Kelly is a lifelong student of world religions, philosophies and ideologies. He earned a Ph.D. in philosophy from Boston University. Kidnapped as a child by a Haitian Voodoo priest and intended as a sacrifice to Pagan gods, he spent his early years in Haiti, went to school in Jamaica, and has spent most of his adult life in the United States, working first as a teacher and subsequently in the computer industry. He is now retired and lives in Colorado.

Index

0-595-21178-X

www.ingramcontent.com/pod-product-compliance
Lightning Source LLC
Chambersburg PA
CBHW020252290526
45784CB00003B/1219